LEADING GOD'S PEOPLE

RICHARD BONDI
LEADING GOD'S PEOPLE

Ethics for the Practice of Ministry

ABINGDON PRESS
Nashville

LEADING GOD'S PEOPLE: ETHICS FOR THE PRACTICE OF
MINISTRY

Copyright © 1989 by Abingdon Press

This book is printed on acid-free paper.

Library of Congress Cataloging-in-Publication Data

Bondi, Richard.
  Leading God's people : ethics for the practice of ministry /
Richard Bondi.
    p. cm.
  Bibliography: p.
  ISBN 0-687-21275-8 (alk. paper)
  1. Clergy—Professional ethics. 2. Christian ethics—Catholic authors.
I. Title.
BV4011.5.B66   1989
241' .641—dc20   89-33143
                                                              CIP

Scripture quotations are from *The New Jerusalem Bible*, copyright © 1985 by
Darton, Longman & Todd, and Doubleday & Company, Inc. Reprinted by
permission of the publishers.

MANUFACTURED BY THE PARTHENON PRESS AT
NASHVILLE, TENNESSEE, UNITED STATES OF AMERICA

CONTENTS

A few years ago, a group of seminary students were sitting in a small circle in a stuffy room, waiting for their weekly supervised ministry reflection seminar to come to an end. Most of them were waiting with more anticipation than usual, because one of them had just raised a question that nobody wanted to talk about. These students were in a field placement at Ebenezer Baptist Church in Atlanta, Georgia. They had been assigned to assist in lobbying the state legislature on issues related to poverty, racism, citizen rights, hunger, and homelessness and had spent the previous week making phone calls or stuffing envelopes, researching state laws, or observing testimony on proposed legislation. The student who spoke up had been assisting in the layout and design of a newsletter linking groups active in support of the homeless. He had made the other students look closely at the clock by saying, "I don't know about the rest of you, but I'm getting tired of wasting my time doing things any volunteer could do. We're supposed to be preparing for the ministry. All these issues we're working on are important, all right, but when I get a church, the people there won't ask me if I'm some kind of moral leader. They'll want to know if I can preach or handle a budget or make a hospital visit. So what's the point of all this, anyway?"

I looked at my watch, too, because I was the faculty supervisor of the group, and the student's question was directed at the seminary through me. His question was more than a complaint about the usefulness of graduation requirements. Nor could it be easily dismissed as a self-deceptive attempt to evade the social-corporate dimensions of his faith. Instead, it reflected his experience of sharply conflicting expectations about the image of "minister" that his training should prepare him to live out. More than that, it reflected genuine confusion about the vocation of Christian ministry as it was understood by his church, his seminary, and himself. Finally, I realized from the embarrassed silence around the room that far from being alone in his frustration, he was simply the one honest enough to say something out loud.

I can't remember what I said to him at the time, but this book is what I would like to say to him now. I hope also to address his sisters and brothers in ministry, as well as those engaged in the theological education and professional training of ministers and lay leaders, and, at least indirectly, the members of the Christian congregations where the risky exercise of leadership takes place. In this book I try to do ethics for the practice of ministry, that is, to engage in critical reflection on the church's mission to increase the love of God and neighbor in the world. My hope is that in doing so others may be better equipped to undertake that reflection themselves, so that, as Paul said many years ago, our "fellowship in faith may come to expression in full knowledge of all the good we can do for Christ" (Philem. 6).

In this effort, I have been encouraged and supported by fellow workers at the Candler School of Theology at Emory University, where I owe special thanks to Romney Moseley and Gail R. O'Day, and by the Emory Catholic Center, whose members even seem to appreciate my sense of humor. Part of the argument of the book had its first hearing at the 1985 annual meeting of the Society of Christian Ethics, where I was greatly aided by a stimulating discussion of my paper. Davis Perkins gave invaluable editorial direction early on in the project, and Ulrike Guthrie helped with the completion of the manuscript. My wife, Roberta, has been my conversation partner and fly-fishing companion, and my stepchildren, Grace and Ben, supported me each in their own inimitable ways. Roberta reminds me to thank our cats, who would occasionally comment on a passage by walking across the keyboard. But I owe my greatest debt to the students, ministers, and laypersons whose stories I tell in what follows. To them, wherever they are, this book is gratefully dedicated.

CHAPTER 1

RESTLESS HEARTS

The Challenge of Moral Leadership

A woman who has been an active and well-known member of her local congregation calls the senior minister to say she and her husband have just separated, and to set up a meeting with the minister for counseling. His first words to her: "Well, for God's sake, don't tell anyone in the church." She hangs up and does not call again.

A rural southern town lies in a smooth bowl of land surrounded by red clay fields. The water supply is controlled by a public utility; for a monthly fee residents get water drawn from a nearby river. There are three artesian wells that are on public land and have never been capped. They are the major source of water for those in poverty who cannot pay the monthly fee; these people are mostly black. Two wells are at opposite ends of the town, another in the center near a church with a white congregation. A prolonged drought occurs, and the wells on the ends of town dry up; the central well, at a lower elevation, still holds water. Impoverished black people begin to come into town to draw water from this well. The white minister of another church in the town, taking a break while preparing his sermon for the week, watches from his window while workers hired by the first church cap the well, which has turned out to be on church property after all. The poor must now walk two miles to carry untreated river water home.

A student pastor in an inner-city church has a friend who left seminary after going public with his homosexuality. The friend comes to the student pastor and asks her assistance in setting up a ministry to AIDS sufferers that would operate out of an unused room in the church-school building. She is eager to help and consults her senior minister. He tells her he hopes she will show every charity to her friend, but letting homosexuals use church property is out of the question.

A woman in her first appointment as an associate minister is present at a social concerns committee meeting. The chief topic of discussion is a proposal that the church should organize a pro-life demonstration at a nearby abortion clinic. One committee member says that she'll go along with the demonstration if the church will also send a delegation to an upcoming vigil at the county courthouse to protest capital punishment. She is hotly accused of being a blackmailer and a communist.

What would it look like for the ministers in these scenes to exercise moral leadership? Where and how would they lead? After all, we live in a world where different stories of what it means to lead a good life compete for our hearts. These stories do not speak with a common voice. More often than not, we hear several at once, each asking us to respond differently. Such competing voices can be heard in the events of ministry just described. Some ask us to respond out of mercy rather than judgment and not to offer stones when people seek bread. Some ask us to protect ourselves and the church and to cast out the sinful who threaten our purity. Some ask us to separate the religious from the secular, the private from the public, and not let one unduly influence the other. Some ask us to speak a prophetic word to those around us, even at the risk of offending them and isolating ourselves.

In saying that we can hear such stories speaking in the events of ministry just described, I am not using "story" to mean "something made up." In fact, I am talking about stories that tell more truth about our lives than we sometimes care to admit. The word "story" can be used to mean many things. We commonly say that every individual or community has a story, an account of how they came to be who or what they are. Everyone's story is different, but we recognize that it is also connected to other people's stories, just as no one lives completely shut off from others. We speak of "my story" and "your story," but also of "our story" and "their story." In fact, every time we tell a particular story, we are selecting from and reinterpreting a whole host of other stories that intersect the one we tell. Stories, just like people's lives, never stand alone.[1]

Stories are woven together in the telling of history, in works like *The Black Family in Slavery and in Freedom* or *Women of Spirit: Female Leadership in the Jewish and Christian Traditions*. The interpretative process is also evident in fictional works based on factual history, like *The Divine Comedy* or *The Name of the Rose*. The weaving of stories in novels like *The Mists of Avalon* or *Monsignor Quixote* allows us to hear our own stories anew by posing imaginative alternatives to the world we inhabit.[2]

But there are also larger stories that go beyond a particular author's historical account or imaginative creation. They are recorded in the folk tales of Africa, Australia, and the Americas, in the holy books of India, China, and Japan, in the Scriptures of Judaism, Christianity, and Islam. Such stories disclose a vision of what the world really is or what it ought to become. They operate on a grand scale to form the frame of self-understanding, not just for individuals but for whole human cultures. They offer models of character and possibilities for the arrangement of human societies. They suggest virtues and vices, depict passions and abiding affections, and offer images for understanding ourselves and the world around us. They give us a goal, a destination, an image of what the world would be like if we shaped ourselves toward the good envisioned by the story. The great stories of the good life can offer radically different lives for us to lead, and they have competed for the allegiance of the human heart since the earliest storytellers told tales of the Great Mother and the Dying and Rising King.[3]

The competition of stories is not limited to the contrasting worlds of the Tao Te Ching, the Qur'an, or the Hebrew and Christian bibles. The great stories themselves are seldom told in one voice and are never free from the constant need for interpretation, as the living stories of women and men are woven with them in the present day. There is no more a harmonious and unitary "Christian story," standing secure without need of interpretation, than there is a single way to tell what we refer to with equal ambiguity as "the story of Western civilization." We may profess that God is One, but we must confess that the stories of God are many.[4]

The associate pastor at the social concerns meeting faced the problem of competing stories. The people present were members of a Christian church, but they were also members of radically different special interest groups, and it was not at all clear that the common story of church membership was in fact basic enough to draw the people together in the face of such divisive issues. She was confronted with the leadership task of moving the two groups present toward a common goal, yet all she had to appeal to was a story that they may not have in common. She may have found herself appealing to a story that did not mean very much to them over against the powerful stories of their separate special interest groups.

The pastor watching the well-capping from his study window also faced competing stories. The Christian story that congregation professed in church on Sunday seemed in sharp contrast with the story of race and class superiority they practiced in well-capping on Monday. The minister was at a loss for what to do. After all, it was not *his* church that capped the well. Why should he feel called to say anything at all? Wouldn't that be interference in the affairs of the other church? Yet a question pulls at his heart as he stands at his window, restlessly suspended between the world of the Gospels he reads and the world of well-capping he must read them in. Perhaps the history of that church and maybe even his own church makes the well-capping understandable, but doesn't the larger story of Jesus that both churches profess make the well-capping morally unacceptable?

It is one of the hallmarks of our age that we have many conflicting stories laying claim to our allegiance and many different interpretations of the stories we are willing to lay claim to ourselves. Our hearts are pulled in many directions by stories that would have us become different kinds of people in order to embody the conflicting truths they contain. The super-apostles at Corinth were impressive with their golden words and wondrous signs, but they tempted the Corinthians to betray the gospel preached by Paul. Martin Luther King's "Letter from Birmingham City Jail" said bluntly that although many Christian ministers had made their peace with segregation, that was not a peace open to a minister of the gospel as he read it. Alan Boesak fiercely lays claim to the Reformed tradition in Christian thought and declares that Afrikaners who call themselves Reformed and practice apartheid are no less than heretics.[5]

We are people shaped by stories of who we are and who we are called to become. We are people of restless hearts, longing for direction and purpose in an uncertain world, for a story that will make sense of our existence, and for leaders who will help us embody that story. Those who would lead us must ultimately appeal to our hearts, calling into being the deepest aspirations of our personal and communal existence and making stories of the good accessible to the hearts of ordinary people. They must make it possible to link "my story" and "your story" with "our story" and "their story," and to connect all those smaller stories with the larger ones that give the world meaning and purpose. This is partly the challenge of telling the story so that it can be heard and partly the challenge of interpreting it truthfully in a particular time and place.

The apostle Paul did this for many of the people of his time and in doing so transformed the way all Christians subsequently would understand themselves in relation to God, church, and world. In our own day, leaders like Martin Luther King, Jr., and Alan Boesak have made such vital connections, breaking down the barriers that prevent people from seeing the solidarity in Christ that ought to lie beyond the fearful separation of "their story" from "our story." All three leaders told the story of Christ in competition with other great stories and with contrasting understandings of the Christian story itself. Each spoke out of a heart restless for a truthful story and found for other restless hearts a destination. How they did so, and how others might do so as well, is the story of the minister as moral leader.

The Edge and the Center

What *is* the story of our hearts? What kind of people does it call us to become? The senior minister counseling his student pastor to extend private mercy, while forbidding her to take a public stand, finds himself conflicted in his very character. Is he the kind of person who is moved by the story of a God who showed mercy to all and who appeared in public with saints and sinners, or is he the kind of person who will defend the interest of his church community not to take a public stand on a controversial issue? He hears both calls, but can he answer both? However difficult such questions might be, I think it is easier for ministers to respond truthfully if they think of themselves as living at the *edge* of their communities rather than at the *center*. I do not mean the geographic edge or center of the community, but the center of stability and propriety that stands in contrast to the edge of change and challenge.

It may seem odd to favor the edge over the center. Many of us have bad memories of being on the "edge" of different groups. Some have felt outcast at the edge of a family or a group of peers in school or at work. Others have been outsiders, living on the fringe of political or economic power, or given second-class status by dominant racial or sexual attitudes. All of these are lonely and isolated places where it is hard to have self-esteem and harder to survive adversity. In contrast, we usually have positive images of "the center." We want to move to the mainstream, to the centers of power and respectability, in order to influence the course of history. On a smaller scale, we may think of being in the center as being surrounded by acceptance and affirmation. We even have in Christian tradition the metaphorical picture of God as the center of the universe toward which all creatures are drawn. In order to see the positive side of living on the edge, we need to see some of the drawbacks to life in the center.

The principal danger we face when we live in the center is that we have too much to lose. Living at the center provides a sense of security and continuity and a more homogeneous way of life, yet these very things endanger us when they become so important that we will defend uncritically the way of life that produces them. They endanger us even more if they become so normal to us, so much the story of what the world is like, that we lose the ability to see the difference between the world we live in and the world our stories of the good call us to bring forth. Living in the center is dangerous because it can tempt us to defend the status quo without thinking. Why ask critical questions when life seems so good?[6]

The minister receiving the phone call from the woman with a troubled marriage is facing this problem. Why is she rocking the boat? She has been a staunch member of the community, working at its center, known to all. Why is she having problems? Doesn't she realize she will be a stumbling block to others, who will question their own lives in watching hers fall apart? The minister may not realize it, but he is engaging in an all-too-typical pattern of blaming the victim for upsetting the story of the good life as it has been defined by the central interests of his community.[7]

Another pernicious danger of life at the center is a sort of idolatry. We tend to substitute our experience in that community for God, or at least to limit "God" to how that community has traditionally pictured the divine. In doing this, *we* become the center of the universe, not God, and we come to judge the stories of God by how much they agree with the stories we tell at our human centers. Ironically enough, it is because Christians do affirm that God is the center of the universe that we cannot affirm that particular human communities have a finally central place in our lives. Movement of some sort is taking place daily in the lives of individuals and communities. Any particular experience of community is only a place along the way that community is traveling. Trying to stay at the center of a community is a lost effort that requires constant denial of the realities of time and change, constant attempts to falsify experience and to turn back the hands of time. In doing this we commit folly at best and idolatry at worst.[8]

The pastor watching the well-capping is experiencing this problem. His parishioners, and those of the church across the street, are all familiar with a theme in the Christian story that tells us to love our neighbors. But who is our neighbor? The church doing the well-capping is interpreting that story from the perspective of the center of their own church community. They are saying, "Those closest to us are our neighbors, so we must act to protect their interests." The pastor watching the workers also wonders who his neighbors are. If they are his own church, should he remain silent so he won't scandalize them? If they are the church across the street, should he remain silent so he won't offend them? Both interpretations look out from the center of his own church community. But what if he looked from the edge of that community? What neighbors would he run into there? Would that encounter lead him to protest the well-capping?

Living on the edge provides a critical angle of vision on the community and an avenue of access to other communities and their stories. It keeps us from thinking that our story is the only story. It constantly challenges the sense of what "our" includes, of who "we" are. It asks us to reinterpret our story in light of our experience on the edge. But more than that, living on the edge leads us to let our stories interpret our experience in a way that the center would find too risky to undertake.

Perhaps the pastor watching the well-capping might turn to the story of the good Samaritan in pondering his own situation. An earnest young man asked Jesus who his neighbor might be and got a characteristically unexpected reply. Far from identifying neighbors close at hand from the center of the community, in his parabolic answer Jesus reaches out beyond the edge of the Jewish community to picture the neighbor not just as a stranger but as one normally despised by those at the center. Even more important, he pictured the Samaritan as a neighbor not by geographic or ethnic proximity but by how he was moved to help the traveler. In contrast to the priest and the Levite who kept to the center of the road, the Samaritan was a neighbor whose heart led him to cross wide boundaries. " 'Which of these three, do you think, proved himself a neighbor to the man who fell into the bandits' hands?' He replied, 'The one who showed pity towards him.' Jesus said to him, 'Go, and do the same yourself' " (Luke 10:36-37). In telling the story, then, Jesus was offering the possibility of transformation. He was suggesting the human movement that is possible when we have an angle of vision on the centers whose defense isolates us from our neighbors.[9]

Yet, perhaps ironically, we can think of life on the edge only in relation to some sort of life at the center. Even the story we just looked at, although told by a leader on the edge, has helped to define the center of those who preserved and handed it down. It became part of the canon of stories that comfort and trouble those who profess to be Christians. Life could be lived on the edge alone only if we were exempt from time and did not have to transmit wisdom as well as genes over many generations. Without some sort of social continuity, great movements would die after birth and have no long-term transforming impact on human communities. Movement that is generated at the edge of a community must finally move the center as well, or it splits off and becomes isolated from the community in which it arose. At the same time, the center that resists movement becomes a dead center. The center without an active edge is as isolated and powerless as the edge without a center.

The pastor at the well-capping faces this problem. He wants to live at the edge but needs the support of the center. Perhaps more than that, he wants to move the center toward the edge without falling off himself. He feels genuinely shocked by the capping and wants to help his own church see the indigent black people who were using the well as neighbors whom they should love. He wants to lead his church to *become* the kind of neighbors Jesus envisioned in the story of the good Samaritan. If he can do this, perhaps he can marshal the political and financial resources of the center on behalf of those on the edge. But he finds himself thinking, "If I take too strong a stand, I'll alienate my church members. They might stop listening to me at all, maybe even try to move me to a different church, and then I couldn't have any impact at all. What should I do?"

The edge and the center are paired in a difficult bond. There is movement and vitality on the edge, but power and stability at the center. Leaders who live only at the edge can become detached from their communities and unable to lead, whereas leaders who commandeer the center can end up protecting its interests from the dangerous opportunities of the edge. Nonetheless, trying to live always at the center is the more dangerous temptation, for stability without movement leads to stagnation and eventual collapse. Defending the center fragments us into smaller and smaller centers, circumscribing our hearts with barriers that isolate what they are trying to defend. Such a situation could end up paralyzing leaders and the communities in which they would lead. What makes movement possible in the face of such paralysis?

The Possibility of Movement

Leadership has to do with the movement of people through time and change. Moral leadership has to do with ensuring that the direction and form of that movement allow people to discover the true destination of their restless hearts and to live that out in a world full of voices calling us to other destinations. The Christian minister as moral leader tries to help Christian communities embody the presence of Christ in the world today, so that we truly reflect the character of the God we profess. But how can we sort out the conflicting stories that would have us respond one way rather than another? How can we find a resting place for our restless hearts?[10]

Communities gather around a story that answers the question, What kind of people are we called to become? We realize that many such stories compete for people's hearts, pulling them into different communities and making personal response and corporate leadership very difficult. Will I be able to move to answer my heart's deepest call, or is the possibility of movement lost in the complex tangle of voices asking me to go one way rather than another?

Part of our difficulty in knowing how to respond is exactly this experience of being called by several stories at once. We live in an age of fragmented lives. It is not simply as if we stand apart from community, hearing voices declaring different destinations and then choosing the one that happens to grip our hearts. In fact, most of us live somewhere on the edge or in the center of several communities, each with differing stories, each with some claim on our hearts. It is hard to generate movement in one direction or another because we find ourselves paralyzed in trying to maintain this delicate balance. It is hard to declare which community we belong to when several lay claims on our hearts.

The student pastor caught between her friend and her pastor feels this sharply. What is her community? To whose story should she respond? To her friend from seminary days? To the church she is presently serving? Is she claimed by her allegiance to the institutional church in which she seeks full ordination? By the people of the city in which she lives? By humankind in general? Or by the Body of Christ throughout the world? She feels confused by these many voices and realizes she cannot answer them all.

The possibility of movement arises when there is conflict between life as people have come to describe it and life as they actually begin to experience it. Such a discrepancy opens possibilities for movement as people need new stories, or fresh interpretations of their old stories, to make sense of the shifting world around them. Movement out of confusion and paralysis arises from the often painful consciousness of conflict. Thus, it is all the more important for ministers to live on the edge of their communities, because there is a greater likelihood that conflict will first appear and be recognized at the edge, whereas the center, with more to defend, will be tempted to resist change and to falsely harmonize discordant stories. However painful it might be, the experience of being claimed by more than one community is a good thing, for it keeps leaders on the edge and forces them to ask critical questions about where the stories of each community would have them lead and whether there are larger stories still that might cast new light on the conflict in question.[11]

The student pastor might feel compelled to choose her friend over her vocation as a minister, but she might also come to see her vocation in a different light from that in which her senior pastor sees his. She might hear her vocation calling her to serve the needs of her friend in a way that will put her in conflict with the institutional church and the expectations of her parishioners. In doing this, she may serve as a catalyst, calling into question the moral adequacy of the stories of church and parish and generating movement toward a deeper understanding of the story of Christ.

The woman calling her minister about her marriage is also facing conflict. To her the world has become a place of chaos. The story of the good life she had been living no longer makes sense of her experience. Her marriage is shattered, her social status in the community threatened, her economic livelihood endangered. She seeks refuge in the story offered by her church. Perhaps here order can be made out of chaos, and her conflicts resolved. Yet she finds her minister describing the world as a place of order where *she* is the threat of chaos. Cut loose from the story of the middle-class church, as she was from the story of the middle-class marriage, she leaves them both, adrift between communities, awash in conflict.

The consciousness of conflict in her life revealed the inadequacy of two interpretative stories, those of the middle-class marriage and the middle-class church. Her painful awareness of conflict opens the possibility of genuine movement in her life. It demands the reinterpretation of what it means to be married and of what it means to be a Christian. She found herself dangerously on the edge of her most significant communities and turned to a member of one of them for this reinterpretation. What she became conscious of instead was *further* conflict. The minister failed to recognize her perspective from the edge of the community and reacted by serving the interests of the center, which was threatened by her pain and did not want to let her story enter its own.

Movement occurred here, but not the sort of movement one would have hoped for. The consciousness of conflict creates the *possibility* of movement. In order to be a movement toward hope and not despair, people in conflict must be shown that the world does not have to be the way they presently experience it. In this sense, leaders are always engaged in consciousness-raising. They raise consciousness about the concrete situation of the people they want to lead, about what stories are actually functioning in a fundamental way for them, and about what those stories have to say to the situation at hand. They begin this consciousness-raising at the point of conflict between expectation and experience, at the fault line between what is and what might be. In doing so they offer people a way to move toward an alternative world that shows them how to integrate the desires of their hearts with the truths of their existence.[12]

But what should those desires be? Which stories reveal the truths of existence? Which ones offer only terrible fantasies? Although conflict raises the possibility of movement, it makes the direction of movement all the more difficult to discern. We might be tempted by stories that tell us we can avoid all conflicts or quickly and easily resolve any that arise. We might be tempted not to listen to the deeper voices of the stories that claim our hearts, when those voices would force us to reconsider whether we were truly embodying the vision of the good of which they speak.

Each of the ministers we have looked at faces this temptation. The minister answering the phone finds it much easier to silence the troubled woman than to face conflict in the church. The minister watching the well-capping can easily justify his own silence by telling himself he can do more good in a community undisrupted by conflict. The student pastor can tell herself she must listen to her senior pastor and not take a public stance on a controversial issue (as her senior pastor tells himself he must listen to his congregation and his institutional church). Finally, the associate pastor at the social concerns meeting can avoid conflict by joining the majority in voting down dissent, saying to herself that, after all, this is a democracy.

The possibility of movement remains just that, only a possibility, without a destination for the journey that movement undertakes. Our hearts may find many stopping places and still remain restless if those destinations do not let us tell a true story about the world and our relations in it. What would such a destination look like?

The Destination of the Heart

One of the great travelers of the heart, Augustine of Hippo, put the problem this way many years ago, addressing God at the beginning of his *Confessions* by crying out, "Our hearts find no peace until they rest in you."[13] The problem of moral leadership in the Christian life is the problem of how to lead people to God and to a life that embodies God in the world. The possibility of movement toward such a destination seems a hopelessly incredible task. Yet we are not without hope, for we move in the company of many others, whose stories give us more than a glimpse of the way. Earlier I spoke of the story of the good Samaritan and of how the minister watching the well-capping might draw on it for clarity of vision in his own situation. We do well to recall that the story of the good Samaritan is told in answer to the question of a restless lawyer.

> And now a lawyer stood up and, to test him, asked, "Master, what must I do to inherit eternal life?" He said to him, "What is written in the Law? What is your reading of it?" He replied, "You must love the Lord your God with all your heart, with all your soul, with all your strength, and with all your mind, and your neighbour as yourself." Jesus said to him, "You have answered right, do this and life is yours." But the man was anxious to justify himself and said to Jesus, "And who is my neighbour?" (Luke 10:25-29)

The stories of Jesus often take a surprising turn. Matthew and Mark also record the Great Commandment, but in their telling of the Christian story it occurs in the context of wrangling with Scribes and Pharisees, as they try to trip Jesus up about fine points of the Mosaic law. That context is visible in Luke's account, but it recedes, bringing the lawyer's quest to the fore. He tries to test Jesus, but Jesus turns his question around and tests him, drawing from him the double command to love God and neighbor. The lawyer persists, asking, "And who is my neighbor?" Jesus responds with the story of the good Samaritan, which the lawyer must have considered a dangerously concrete image of how to embody the Great Commandment. The lawyer must have felt at the same time chastened, enlightened, and challenged far beyond what he had expected when he began the exchange.[14]

Over thirty years ago H. Richard Niebuhr, in a profound mediation on the purpose of the church and its ministry, came to a conclusion that rings just as true today as it did then: "When all is said and done the increase of this love of God and neighbor remains the purpose and the hope of our preaching of the gospel, of all our church organization and activity, of all our ministry, of all our efforts to train [men and women] for the ministry, of Christianity itself."[15]

Niebuhr depicts a church that would lead restless hearts to God, their destination. His vision moves from the proclamation of the gospel, through its institutional transmission, through the general ministry of all Christians, through the formation of ministers in community, and finally returns to Christianity as a whole, making the double love of God and neighbor not something accidental but essential. It is the natural response of those shaped by the story of Jesus to become in their own time and place the kind of people called to be the Body of Christ in the world and to embody this presence in a ministry rooted in, sustained by, and drawn toward the increase of the love of God and neighbor.

Like the lawyer in the passage from Luke, those who would embody the command today must also ask questions whose answers might be very unsettling indeed. We still ask, "Who is my neighbor?" as the minister watching the well-capping discovered. But we have other questions also, as we journey on our own quest and try to lead other restless hearts. Whose story do I tell? Is it the gospel of Christ, or the gospel of personal power, of institutional preservation, of cultural accommodation? Whose truth do I teach? Is it the revelation of the Spirit, nurtured over time and continually testing the limits of human language, or is it the current or traditional dogma or ideology? Whose care do I seek? Is it the care of God the creator given to the needy of creation, or is it the largesse of the privileged that is given so that the giver might prosper? Whose table do I set? Is it the Lord's Supper, where the broken are healed and the hungry filled with good things, or is it the banquet of Dives, with Lazarus kept starving outside the gate? Where does my allegiance lie? Do I serve the One who took the form of a slave, or do I serve those who promise that one day I too will be a master?

The struggle involved in trying to answer these questions

requires constant moral reflection in the life of the church and the lives of its ministers. Whatever else a minister is, at the heart of her or his vocation is the call to be a moral leader. The overriding question of Christian ministry is not *whether* leadership will arise. It is, rather, *what kind* of leadership will arise and *where* it will lead the Body of Christ.

Moral leadership is not a separate office of ministry or a specialty of the profession practiced by some and not by others. The minister as moral leader is called to assist the restless people of God in moving ever closer to the destination of their hearts. This destination is not the endpoint of a journey but the way of the journey itself. It is the way shown by Jesus, who commanded us to love God and neighbor and gave us a terrifyingly beautiful example of the lengths we must go to in showing that love.

In the pages ahead, we will explore the vocation of the minister and the possibility of a ministry that transforms leaders and followers alike. We will look more closely at how the minister as moral leader tells the story of the good in the center and on the edge of her or his community. We will consider the temptation not to lead and the temptation to betray. We will close with a look at those virtues of life on the edge that best suit us for the faithful pursuit of the Great Commandment. In all this we must keep our eyes firmly fixed on the true destination of our restless hearts. The love of God and the love of neighbor are as one. The service of God and neighbor that we call ministry is a service united in its source and its goal, in our call to it, and in the kind of people we are called to become: a holy people, whose hearts are filled with love.

CHAPTER 2

HEARING THE CALL

Meanwhile Saul was still breathing threats to slaughter the Lord's disciples. He went to the high priest and asked for letters addressed to the synagogues in Damascus, that would authorize him to arrest and take to Jerusalem any followers of the Way, men or women, that he might find.

It happened that while he was travelling to Damascus and approaching the city, suddenly a light from heaven shone all round him. He fell to the ground, and then he heard a voice saying, "Saul, Saul, why are you persecuting me?" "Who are you, Lord?" he asked, and the answer came, "I am Jesus, whom you are persecuting. Get up and go into the city, and you will be told what you are to do." The men travelling with Saul stood speechless, for though they heard the voice they could see no one. Saul got up from the ground, but when he opened his eyes he could see nothing at all, and they had to lead him into Damascus by the hand. For three days he was without his sight and took neither food nor drink.

There was a disciple in Damascus called Ananias, and he had a vision in which the Lord said to him, "Ananias!" When he replied, "Here I am, Lord," the Lord said, "Get up and go to Straight Street and ask at the house of Judas for someone named Saul, who comes from Tarsus. At this moment he is praying, and has seen a man called Ananias coming in and laying hands on him to give him back his sight."

But in response, Ananias said, "Lord, I have heard from many people about this man and all the harm he has been doing to your holy people in Jerusalem. He has come here with a warrant from the chief priests to arrest everybody who invokes your name." The Lord replied, "Go, for this man is my chosen instrument to bring my name before gentiles and kings and before the people of Israel; I myself will show him how much he must suffer for my name." Then Ananias went. He entered the house, and laid his hands on Saul and said, "Brother Saul, I have been sent by the Lord Jesus, who appeared to you on your way here, so that you may recover your sight and be filled with the Holy Spirit." It was as though scales fell away from his eyes and immediately he was able to see again. So he got up and was baptized, and after taking some food he regained his strength. (Acts 9:1-19*a*)

The story of the conversion of Paul and his mission to the Gentiles was so important to the early Christian communities that we find it told four times in the Scriptures: Acts 9:1-19*a*, Acts 22:1-16, Acts 26:9-18, and Galatians 1:12-24. The accounts differ in who tells the story (Acts 9 has Luke, the rest have Paul), who is its audience (respectively, the readers of Acts, the Jews in Jerusalem, Roman officials, and the readers of Galatians), and some important details (Acts 9 and 22 have the Lord speaking to Ananias, who then informs Paul of his mission, whereas Acts 26 has the Lord speaking directly to Paul, and Galatians assumes the Lord spoke but records no speech). Although they cannot be harmonized, they agree in telling a story pivotal for early Christianity: Paul of Tarsus, who once thought it his duty "to use every means to oppose the name of Jesus the Nazarene," received a personal call "not from any human being" but "through a revelation of Jesus Christ" and became the Lord's "chosen instrument," a "witness before all humanity," "so that they may turn from darkness to light," "urging them to repent and turn to God, proving their change of heart by their deeds."[1]

Many years later a woman we can call Linda was born, the first child of a mother who taught grade school and a father who sold appliances in a small department store in the Midwest. Her parents were members of Pleasant Grove Baptist Church. Linda went to Sunday school, where she excelled at memorizing Scripture, and was baptized during a revival when she was fourteen years old. She graduated from high school and went to the state university, intending to complete a degree in secondary education. In her sophomore year she became involved with another student, got pregnant, and stayed home after Christmas break, where she had a dangerous miscarriage in January and was hospitalized for three weeks. During this time her parents had remained supportive, though they were bitterly disappointed in her, but most of the people in her old church acted as if she were invisible. She spent the rest of the semester recovering at home and in June moved permanently to a city near the university. The next school year she enrolled again as an accounting major, and eventually she graduated with honors.

Linda lived on her own for several years and became a successful accountant in a medium-sized firm. She began dating for the first time since college and met a man named Michael whom she liked very much. Michael invited her to come to Mass with him at Sts. Peter and Paul Catholic Church, where he belonged. She became fascinated with the liturgical life of the church, which seemed so very different from the church of her youth. She married Michael, and though she did not officially become a Catholic, more and more of their life centered around the church. They joined a small group that met weekly for prayer and undertook social service projects in the local community.

A year or two passed, and in this time Linda came to realize that her work at church was more real and satisfying than her job at the accounting firm. Each Sunday grew more difficult as she saw the priest at the altar and imagined herself there; each Monday more dissatisfying as she returned to her desk instead of staffing the shelter for the homeless that Sts. Peter and Paul had recently opened. Her tension was plain for all to see, and one evening in their prayer group another woman prayed aloud that Linda would have the strength to respond to the call she was hearing. Linda was stunned. She had never thought of her discomfort in those terms and was afraid of the implications. She and Michael talked things over for a long time with the members of the prayer group and with the priests and sisters at the church. After much prayer and reflection, Linda decided she really was being called. This was a bittersweet realization, for neither the church of her youth nor the church of her adult life was officially receptive to the idea of a woman minister. Nonetheless, she decided at the age of twenty-eight to leave her job and enter a Master of Divinity program at a local Methodist seminary that admitted students of all denominational affiliations. Linda and Michael still attend their Catholic prayer and social service group regularly, but along with her upcoming entry into the Methodist seminary, they are visiting an Episcopal church to see if they can find a spiritual home in a denomination where she has a chance to become a minister.

Paul and Linda seem unlike in many ways. Linda did not grow up persecuting Christians; Paul did not grow up in the church. Linda was not blinded by Christ and given a commission to all humanity; Paul did not come to a slow realization over a long time of a calling to serve God and others. Paul, of course, did not know Linda; but Linda will no doubt find Paul inspiring and exasperating at the same time! Yet they are in many ways alike. Once the call was heard, neither could resist it, wherever it led them. Both will encounter others who question the authenticity or legitimacy of their calls. Both feel caught between God, on the one hand, and the fragmented and often divisive elements of the "church," on the other.

We do not invent ministry anew in each generation. Rather, we inherit an understanding of the call to ministry that is heavily influenced by how people have practiced it in the past. In the stories of Paul and Linda, we can see some things that affect the formation of ministers in any Christian community, shaping our perceptions about what ministry is, who might be called to do it, and how it might be done. Looking at how people hear the call and understand it through inherited images will be an important part of discovering how ministers might carry out the task of moral leadership that the vocation of ministry sets before them.

For much of Christian history, an individual's entry into ministry has been thought of as the personal response to a call. We see this in Paul's roadside conversation with Jesus, but it also lies behind Linda's gradual understanding that she was beckoned to a new life. However the call "happens," it is intensely, sometimes frightfully personal in the changes it makes in the ordinary circumstances of human lives. In Paul's need to defend the authenticity of his commission, and in Linda's painful awareness that her call would not be recognized by the churches she had belonged to, we see the call to ministry putting people out on a lonely road.

Yet although it is personal, the call is not simply private, for it is shaped by the community in which it takes place. Luke was very careful to put Paul's calling in a community context. Paul was with companions on the road; he needed their help to get into Damascus; he prayed and fasted until Ananias came to heal him and deliver God's message; he immediately began to take an active part in preaching the gospel he had so recently persecuted. Linda may not have realized she had had a call if it had not been for her prayer group, and once she accepted the realization, she had to rely on her local church community to help her decide how best to respond to the call. She was also dependent on the official attitudes of her church toward women ministers, and this forced her to respond by trying to find another community in which her call to leadership could be lived out.

The call to ministry also has an institutional dimension that goes beyond its setting in the local communities of those who are called. The institutional church, whether it appears as a national or international denomination or a small rural congregation, tries to shape the personal call into a form acceptable to the traditional understanding of ministry in the faith community that institution represents. The church can impose rules of ministry and roles for the minister through this corporate judgment and can exercise a lot of control over what constitutes a valid call, simply in whom it decides to ordain or employ.

Even at the beginnings of Christianity, Paul experienced this in hearing his call. He claimed to be an apostle but had to defend this claim against the Jewish Christians in Jerusalem and in Galatia. He did not meet the criteria those groups had established for apostolicity, and he differed sharply on the role of the Law in the life of the Christian. But the young church, not Paul, had the last word. Luke, writing later, vigorously defends Paul's call and his mission to the Gentiles but smooths over his sharp differences with the Jewish Christians in the interest of a demonstration of church unity.

Linda certainly feels the constraints of the institutional church in responding to her call. She has met the church in a series of churches—Baptist, Catholic, Methodist, Episcopal—each with its own understanding of what "the call" is, who can hear it, and what sort of leadership it authorizes the hearer to undertake. She could say with Paul that her call came "not by human beings nor through any human being but by Jesus Christ and God the Father who raised him from the dead" (Gal. 1:1), but she is going to have to make the case for the validity of her call before a corporate church body, just as much as Paul did.

We can move closer to capturing Paul's and Linda's complex experience by speaking of their response to the call as a *vocation*. A vocation is a calling to a life work. It is not simply a calling to a life *of* work but a calling to a *specific* sort of work made particular by the stories that characterize the meaning and purpose of the task to which the vocation calls us. The call to love God and neighbor goes out to all people, but it is heard by some as a vocation to take up as a life work the organized task of increasing the love of God and neighbor in the world.[2]

For those who answer the call, the vocation of ministry can become their heartfelt response to the story of God in Christ. It is intensely personal, as it is the response of a particular heart, yet it is always communal since that response leads one out into community and because the images of what kind of minister the vocation would lead a person to become are carried in the stories of a community. As we will see in this book, through reflection on the ministry of Paul and other Christian leaders, the narratives of past vocations kept alive in Christian communities help shape the characters of those responding to the call today, and with it the shape of the vocations they will live out.[3]

A vocation is at the same time a call and a task, a commission and a mission. Luke and Paul agree in this. Paul's calling by God was at the same time his sending to humanity. To be converted was to undertake a vocation at the same time, to engage in a life work that expressed who Paul was as an individual and what Christianity was to become in the world. Linda experiences this also, but with a difference. She has a call but must discern what task it brings in the context of two thousand years of fragmented interpretation of the proper vocation of the Christian and the appropriate shape of the ministry. She may find her call leading her to a vocation that pushes at the boundaries of the institutional self-understanding she encounters. This is a fearful task, though she might find some comfort from the way Paul challenged the self-understanding of the church of his day and in the stories of other women whose vocations challenge the conventional wisdom about the shape of Christian ministry.[4]

Vocations are individual callings confirmed and lived out in communities. Where individuals and communities strongly disagree over the presence or direction of a vocation, there exists the possibility for everything from personal tragedy to communal redefinition. This is precisely one of the tensions that should keep ministers living on the edge of their communities, as they feel their call being shaped by but also pushing against the community traditions in which they try to live it out. Because vocations are both personal and communal, they shape and express the character of individuals and communities, wrestling back and forth to embody the story of the good that claims their hearts. How Paul lived out his vocation had an enormous impact on the character of Christianity. How Linda will live out hers will likely not have such a cosmic impact, but it will be part of a larger struggle determining the self-understanding and mission of the church today.

The shaping of vocation by stories told in community is closely connected with the challenge of moral leadership. How can we lead if we don't know why we'd like to try in the first place, or how we would go about doing it? We find some help in answering these questions in looking at the images of the minister we have inherited from the past. These images tell stories about the character of a minister and the tasks of ministry. They go a long way toward determining whether we hear a call in the first place, what our response will be, and whether it will equip us to lead restless people toward the destination of their hearts.

Inherited Images

In the broadest sense possible, ministry is the active presence of the Body of Christ in the world, as it seeks to respond to the call to love God and neighbor. Our inheritance as Christians includes a number of images of the minister, rooted in the larger Christian story, that in some way or another make sense across church boundaries. Such images figure importantly in a person's response to the vocation of ministry and help shape the institutional offices of ministry in the different churches.[5] In recent years there have been attempts to arrive at an overarching image to meet the challenges of contemporary ministry. "Pastoral Director," "Shepherd," "Pastoral Interpreter," "Practical Theologian," "Partners in the Household of Faith," and "Co-Creators in the New Creation" have each emphasized important aspects of the complex vocation of ministry.[6]

I am not proposing "the Minister as Moral Leader" as a competitive alternative to those images. Rather, I am claiming that *whatever* images one selects, the task of moral leadership is part and parcel of the vocation those images seek to represent. The images of the minister we will examine, therefore, must not be separated from the task of the minister as moral leader. Fulfilling the vocation of moral leadership, in fact, will require the appropriation of many images of the minister, as ministers become all things to all people in order to tell the Christian story truthfully and forcefully in their own place and time. I am suggesting that those who would be ministers will find themselves dwelling on at least the following images in exploring the questions of moral leadership we asked at the end of the last chapter. "Whose story do I tell?" asks the *preacher*. "Whose truth do I teach?" asks the *teacher*. The *pastor* asks, "Whose care do I seek?" whereas the *priest* asks, "Whose table do I set?" Finally, the *servant* wonders, "Where does my allegiance lie?" as conflicting stories compete for a heart called to love. Together these images give shape to the call to a vocation of leadership in the Body of Christ.

If the story is to be heard it must be proclaimed, and from the beginning *preacher* has been one of the fundamental images of the minister. Luke records that Paul lost no time taking up this task. "After he had spent only a few days with the disciples in Damascus, he began preaching in the synagogues, 'Jesus is the Son of God'" (Acts 9:20). Paul himself tells us

"[God] called me through his grace and chose to reveal his Son in me, so that I should preach him to the Gentiles" (Gal. 1:15-16). As preacher, the minister proclaims, evokes, and interprets the Word, trying to make the Christian story accessible, powerful, and understandable in a particular setting.[7]

Because of the importance of this task and the potential power of the pulpit, a question is raised that all preachers must ask: *"Whose story do I tell?"* The ministers we met in chapter 1 watching the well-capping and attending the social concerns meeting will face this question when they prepare their next sermons, as they try to proclaim the Word to their congregations in a time of controversy over what it means to be a Christian community. The minister who drove off the woman facing marital separation and the pastor advising his associate to deny the public requests of her gay parishioner also need to ask themselves this question, lest the image of the preacher they embody be an image shaped by the center of their communities, in isolation from the edge.

Perhaps those ministers feel they have asked and answered that question already. At that point, "Whose story do I tell?" becomes a question for preacher and congregation alike. Is the image of the preacher faithfully reflected in the person and word of the minister? This is not a question that can be answered by the minister alone. Here we are reminded of the communal shaping of the vocation of ministry. Although the individual hears and responds to the call to minister, that call is transmitted and that ministry carried out in community. Neither the minister nor the community is the sole judge of the truthfulness of the ministry. Minister and congregation must always ask themselves whose story they tell in their preaching and hearing of the Word.

Would that there were an easy answer to this question! From the beginning, Paul wrestled with other preachers about the truth of what they were preaching. "However, when Cephas came to Antioch, then I did oppose him to his face since he was manifestly in the wrong" (Gal. 2:11). Yet he struggled just as much with getting his fledgling communities to be responsible for judging the truth of what they heard preached. "You stupid people in Galatia! After you have had a clear picture of Jesus Christ crucified, right in front of your eyes, who has put a spell on you?" (Gal. 3:1). Like the other images to follow, when lived out faithfully, the image of the preacher guarantees the sort of conflict that provides the possibility of moral leadership. These inherited images may not provide answers, but they put both minister and congregation in a position where both must discern the destination of their hearts, and they provide at least a hint of where to move.

The story the preacher proclaims must be transmitted from one generation to the next and made understandable in places far removed from its original language and setting. The minister as *teacher* has performed these functions of education and critical reflection within Christian communities. As teachers, ministers interpret and uphold the truths of the faith, help define the boundaries of traditional understandings, and test the faithfulness of contemporary reinterpretations. We may be more familiar with the teaching function as it has been carried out by the institutional church or through the ministry of professional theologians, but any minister can expect to face questions about the faith or be asked to provide instruction in it. From the teaching of the twelve apostles to last week's Sunday school, the church wrestles with the transmission of the faith.[8]

The image of the teacher is prey to a number of difficulties. It can so commit itself to the defense of a particular generation's answers to questions of belief and behavior that it abandons critical reflection and thus turns education into mere indoctrination. This is certainly something that Linda faces in responding to her call, as the teaching of the Baptist church of her youth and the Catholic church of her maturity defends a doctrine of the maleness of Christ and prevents women from seeking official positions of ministry.

The teacher is also tempted to value conformity over diversity, the center over the edge, in sorting out the many voices in the Christian story. Teaching, in fact, represents a legitimate defense of the center, insofar as it assists in handing down the story without which neither the edge *nor* the center would be comprehensible. Yet the more difficult it is to express and embody the Christian story, the more tempted we become to enforce a uniform reading of it and to suspect interpretations challenging that reading. This temptation is certainly present in the minister who rejects the woman in marital anguish and in the minister reluctant to provide public assistance to a controversial group. But it seems a particular problem for institutions and is a perennial source of friction between institutions and individuals as they struggle with the image of teacher. And when theologians and church officials dispute, it is most often the individual minister who is caught in the crossfire, unsure of whom to trust in telling the story.

Disputes over what constitutes a true telling of the story of Christ represent an ancient and immensely difficult problem. Paul wrestled with it in Jerusalem, Galatia, Corinth, and elsewhere. Such friction is one of the chief causes of the denominational fragmentation of the Body of Christ and of bitter disputes within denominations. Perhaps the most serious outcome of such contests is when theological positions become abstracted from the complex stories in which they are embedded, when giving the "right" answers becomes more important than prayerful reflection on the call to be a certain kind of people in the accidents of our own history, when obedience alone become a substitute for the risky love of God and neighbor.[9]

Thus, the image of the teacher also addresses a question to those who would fill it and to the community in which it is filled. It requires the teacher to ask, *Whose truth do I teach?"* Is it the complicated truth of the story of Christ or the formulaic ideology of a particular generation or social class? The love of truth is a disposition to keep traveling in the light of the vision whose story leads us on and to trust that our discernment is led by the spirit of truth.[10] The critical question posed by the image of the teacher helps equip us for that journey by keeping alive questioning itself. It reminds us of the answers given in the past and gives us a fresh vocabulary to ask them with today. The image of the teacher is essential for the minister as moral leader because education in the breadth of the Christian story and critical reflection on its implications in today's world are important steps in discerning the direction of movement the

People of God are called to undertake. All ministers may not be teachers in a professional sense, but all ministers teach in the daily performance of their ministry and must therefore continually ask themselves whose truth it is they are teaching.

On that journey, because we are social creatures whose lives are always formed in relation to one another and because the Christian story calls us to love God and neighbor, we need for certain members of our communities to be charged with concern for the manner of our living together and the course of our lives in the world. The image of the minister as *pastor* brings into focus the governance and care of the Body of Christ in helping Christian communities to live together in love.[11]

The image of the pastor, with its twin concerns of order and care, has been difficult to embody from the beginning. We find Paul asking the Corinthians, "What do you want then? Am I to come to you with a stick in my hand or in love, and with a spirit of gentleness?" (I Cor. 4:21). There are widely different answers in different church communities to the question of what church order most faithfully represents the Body of Christ in the world today and what sort of care for others best serves the love of God and neighbor. We must not lose sight of the fact that order should be the vehicle of care, though it is very tempting to defend order for its own sake and to forget that the pastor must not only guide others but also respond to their needs.

The minister who admonished the woman not to tell anyone about her marital problems is certainly facing this temptation. He would rather uphold a certain notion of order in the church community than put that order at risk in giving care. The opposition that Linda runs into from those who would exclude women from full participation in the church comes at least in part from male pastors facing this temptation. In opening up the church to women, they would be creating the opportunity for more ministers to serve more needs, but they would also be putting their own positions in the church order at risk.

If order is a vehicle for care, then living out the image of the pastor is primarily a matter of vision and response. Whom do we see as needy, and how do we envision a response? Distortions of the image involve a narrowness of vision or a withholding of response that leads to the neglect or denial of pastoral responsibility. We saw this occurring in the parable of the good Samaritan. In contrast to the unexpected benefactor, the priest and the Levite redescribed the scene they encountered, so that other more "pressing" needs called them away from giving care. The minister watching the well-capping also faced a test of vision. Did he see a need in the scene he observed? Could he envision a response? Could he *pastor* his community into his vision of need and response? The minister at the social concerns meeting and the student pastor hearing a plea to assist people with AIDS could certainly see needs abounding. Their difficulty was how to envision a response appropriate to all the needs present, when any response might challenge church order.

Thus, the critical question asked by the pastor is *"Whose care do I seek?"* Whose needs are served and how care for those needs is defined are powerful issues. Indeed, they are precisely issues of power, and all too often those with power are the ones who have their needs met, while the pastor is blind to the needs of the powerless. The minister telling the woman with marital problems to be quiet may really be responding to the need of powerful members of the community not to have the boat rocked.

It is not easy to know with Paul when to bring a stick or when to bring a spirit of gentleness, or to what end either might be applied. In this respect, it is particularly important to keep governance and care united in the same image and to ensure that this image of pastor is held in balance with other images of the minister. The separation of pastoral functions into images of administrator/bishop and pastoral counselor and the isolation of those from other images makes it possible to forget that church order should be the vehicle of care or it loses its reason for being. Recent critics of the hierarchical structure of most Christian churches have exactly this point in mind when they call for the transformation of an impersonal, authority-loving church toward a relational, care-giving community.[12] Keeping alive the question "Whose care do I seek?" helps pastors check the vision that guides the hand of care *and* governance.

The conflicting needs that surface in any community remind us that human beings are prone to separation. Our deep desire for union competes with our tendency to mistrust others. We are kept apart by common needs that demand scarce resources, separated by unresolved conflict over the aim and purpose of our life together, and divided by our difficulties in speaking across barriers of culture, race, gender, class, and language. The image of the *priest* ministers to our brokenness and separation in the possibility of mediation and reconciliation it offers.[13]

This possibility is based primarily on the role of the priest in the worship life of the community. Some sort of priestly office, conducting rituals that connect the human and divine, is a widespread feature in the history of religions. In Christianity, the priest reenacts the role of Christ as mediator and reconciler between God and humanity. Presiding at the Lord's Supper (whether this is understood as a Eucharist or a memorial service), the priest sets the table at which God and humanity sit as one, and this ritual activity becomes the basis for practical mediation and reconciliation as well.

The image of the priest has been somewhat obscured, because in much of the theology that emerged from the Reformation, the preaching of the Word tended to dominate the service of the Table. "Priest" became associated with high-church ecclesiology and institutional authority. The architecture of churches reflected this imbalance, with "preaching" churches physically centered on the pulpit and "priestly" churches on the altar. Even the practice of the Lord's Supper, passed on to us in I Corinthians 11:17-34 by no less a preacher than Paul, became less and less common in many churches. While the origins of this imbalance are understandable, it remains fundamentally wrong. Preaching is not the only way the Christian story is told. The story is a complex narrative that includes worship, prayer, and sacraments. The imbalance of preaching and worship is a dangerous situation, for it threatens the full and free telling of the story of the community and puts undue emphasis on the personality of the preacher.

Exactly because the priest participates in a ritual that has roots independent of the local church, she or he belongs in the community and yet also has a place outside it. It is this solidarity and separation that allow the priest to connect the local community with larger ones outside it, whether this means a Lutheran priest or a Methodist minister mediating between a local church and a national denomination, or a Catholic bishop in El Salvador trying to reconcile the government and a people's revolutionary army. The image of the priest should be seen on the edge. It connects the sacred and the secular and bridges one group of people to another. In this sense, especially when joined with the other images of the minister, ministers perform priestly mediation and reconciliation even in denominations that do not call them "priests" or where the religious ritual is far more limited than in high sacramental traditions.[14]

The priest lives at the edge by working at the point where communities intersect. This is only strengthened by the fact that priests also live at the center of the community's ritual through their role in worship. When that ritual is kept alive, it competes with the centers formed by human self-interest and secular culture. The ritual center and the social center may well be at odds, keeping alive the sort of conflict out of which moral leadership can arise. This is the situation Paul addressed in Corinth, when he sharply points out how the Lord's Supper condemns the self-satisfied suppers of some of the Corinthians.

> So, when you meet together, it is not the Lord's Supper that you eat; for when the eating begins, each of you has his own supper first, and there is one going hungry while another is getting drunk. Surely you have homes for doing your eating and drinking in? Or have you such disregard for God's assembly that you can put to shame those who have nothing? What am I to say to you? Congratulate you? On this I cannot congratulate you. (I Cor. 11:20-22)

Nonetheless, the image of the priest is subject to distortions. The role of the priest as presider at the communal ritual can become an occasion for personal glorification. Priests can confuse *acting for* Christ with *being* Christ, when they imagine themselves to be the irreplaceable core of the community. Congregations can be held hostage by their need for the priestly functions. They may not oppose priests who lord it over them or churches that elevate priesthood out of proportion to other images, for fear of having the sacramental ministry of mediation and reconciliation withheld. Priests can become too comfortably entrenched at the social rather than the ritual center of their communities. Not wishing to incur anyone's displeasure, or trying to be well liked by everyone, they may fail to risk the separation necessary to act as a genuine mediator and reconciler and end up acting chiefly as an agent of the status quo. The minister responding to the woman facing marital separation and the senior pastor telling his student pastor not to take a public stand about AIDS have lost sight of the image of the priest just as much as they have taken a narrow view of the image of the pastor.

Churches that have emphasized the image of the priest have had special difficulty in coming to terms with the transforming role of women in the church, as Linda has discovered to her pain. At the same time that she has been called into the vocation of ministry by the image of the priest, she has been told that because Jesus was male, only men can be priests. But the central symbolism of the priesthood of Christ is surely that of mediation and reconciliation, rather than maleness. Problems with the priestly image are not found only in those traditions where maleness has been given explicit (if misguided) symbolic importance. For example, even churches that have ordained women for years often have a difficult time putting them in positions of genuine leadership. On a deeper level, churches realize that once women are ordained *and* given significant roles in ministry, irrevocable changes in the church will follow. The same dynamic surrounds the ordination of people from racial, ethnic, and sexual minorities, as well as more serious lay participation in the planning and performance of liturgical celebrations. A truly inclusive priesthood would symbolize a radical healing of brokenness in church and world.

Nonetheless, the image of the priest asks those who would

embody it a critical question that can safeguard it from personal and institutional distortion: *"Whose table do I set?"* Priests must always ask, as Paul did, if it is indeed the Lord's Supper they announce. Who in fact are the guests called to the table? Is the table set with the food and drink of Christ's mediation and reconciliation?

The priestly office is highly symbolic, and the symbol appropriately transcends the person who represents it. The nature of the image should constantly remind both priest and community that the trappings of power, institutional loyalty, or even remarkable personal strengths and weaknesses must not prevent the symbol of Christ as mediator and reconciler from appearing in the midst of the particular time and place in which the priest is called to minister. Only when the priest remains transparent to the symbol of Christ is the priestly office well and truly filled and the Lord's table set for the feast that offers bread, not stone.

The images we have looked at so far, although present in the Christian story and in the vocation of every minister, have a recognizable institutional identity as well. We all know preachers, teachers, pastors, and priests. Christian communions generally do not have an officially designated *servant*. Yet it is fairly common to say about a particular minister that she is a true servant of the gospel, or that he serves his people well.

The Hebrew Scriptures are full of servants, slaves, and even an enigmatic suffering servant. While these images are echoed in the Christian Scriptures, the frequent use Jesus and his followers made of the image was also dependent on the subordinate role of the servant in the hierarchical social system of the day. Jesus effectively turned the values of that system upside down, identifying himself with the lowly servant and rejecting the notion of lording it over other people. That this was understood to be important by early Christians is certainly visible in the letter to the Philippians, where Paul quotes a very early hymn presenting the image of Jesus as servant and commending it as a model to other Christians.

> Nothing is to be done out of jealousy or vanity; instead, out of humility of mind everyone should give preference to others,

everyone pursuing not selfish interests but those of others. Make your own the mind of Christ Jesus:

Who, being in the form of God,
did not count equality with God
something to be grasped.

But he emptied himself,
taking the form of a slave,
becoming as human beings are.

(Phil. 2:3-7)

But simply standing the conventional master-servant relation on its head was not enough. Paul and other early Christians realized that although servants do serve, the real question is *whom* do they serve. Paul forced his readers to ask themselves to whom or what they were bound. He opens Romans by identifying himself as "Paul, a servant of Christ Jesus" (Rom. 1:1). Much of this powerful letter is built on the contrast between the freedom of those who serve the gospel and the hopelessness of those who serve the Law. At its close, Paul adds an admonition against false teachers, saying that "people of that sort are servants not of our Lord Christ, but of their own greed" (Rom. 16:18).

The force of this use of the image of servant is not that servants are intrinsically better than masters but that *all* people need to reject the temptation to be masters, and need to question what ends they serve in their lives. The reign of God makes all human reigns relative. "If I, then, the Lord and Master, have washed your feet, you must wash each other's feet. I have given you an example so that you may copy what I have done to you" (John 13:14-15).

That example has proved inspiring and exasperating in Christian history. The word "minister" itself means "one who serves." But our culture values masters over servants just as much as the Hellenistic world did, though the lines between master and servant are less noticeably drawn. Whether a minister today works in a twenty-five member nondenominational congregation or in the worldwide Roman Catholic church, there is often an important qualification to the image of servant that the minister is urged to adopt. The minister is told that all Christians may be called to be servants, but some serve others first. Local congregations and large churches may treat their ministers like their personal servants, whose loyalty they command, as if Jesus had never washed Peter's feet. The call to servanthood may be nothing more than a call to obedience in the interests of the status quo. Such a call is particularly threatening to women in ministry, for our culture has too often cast them in the role of subservient servant in their other relationships as well.

In fact, the image of servant has often been mediated through the image of an employee. Employees have jobs whose tasks are set by others. The employee, whether a youth minister in a large suburban Methodist church or the Catholic archbishop of an East Coast metropolis, is made subordinate to the institutional needs of the church. The employee strongly feels the temptation to serve the status quo, for the defense of the institution as it has been traditionally maintained preserves whatever social status the minister might have and holds out the hope of rising within the institution to occupy its higher levels and become a "successful servant."[15]

Yet the problem is not that ministers are servants, because, as Paul reminds us, all Christians ought to be. The problem is that when scriptural servants become institutional employees, the pull to the center does fierce battle with a gospel that would turn it upside down, and we play the risky game of trying to please two masters. Here the minister may be caught between serving conscience or serving consequences, and very often only conflict and difficulties will follow.

Furthermore, in the conflict that follows upon challenging Caesar, we must not be misled by an erroneous interpretation of the servant as one who suffers for the sake of suffering. Paul may have dwelt at length on his wounds and his weaknesses, but he was quick to say he could only boast of them (and even then boast as a fool) because he got them as a servant of Christ. "It is, then, about my weaknesses that I am happiest of all to boast, so that the power of Christ may rest upon me; and that is why I am glad of weaknesses, insults, constraints, persecutions, and distress for Christ's sake. For it is when I am weak that I am strong" (II Cor. 12:9-10). That phrase, "for Christ's sake," should remind us that there is a *point* to suffering and that the worth of suffering depends on *why* it is undergone.

Thus, the image of the servant leads a minister to ask, *"Where does my allegiance lie?"* It asks this of institutions as well as individuals, where we recall that the aim of Christian institutions is to carry out the command to love God and neighbor. The answer to this question is no more self-evident than the answers to any of the questions asked by the other images of the minister. But it is a particularly important one because it tempers and qualifies the others. The preacher as servant is helped in answering "Whose story do I tell?" by also asking, "Where does my allegiance lie?" just as the teacher, the pastor, and the priest are also aided in their critical reflection by keeping in mind whom it is they serve.[16]

The minister watching the well-capping feels pressured to serve the interests of the church he pastors *and* to serve the needs of the powerless. In trying to answer "Whose care do I seek?" he will be greatly helped by keeping alive the question "Where does my allegiance lie?" for it will drive him past his local concerns and remind him he serves the God revealed in Christ, whose stories have no place for segregation. The student pastor feels caught between serving her pastor, her church, and her friend. In trying to answer "Whose story do I preach?" she will be helped by reflecting on "Where does my allegiance lie?" and she will discover that she cannot be a servant of the Word and refuse a call for help from "the least" of her brothers and sisters.

It is little wonder that being a servant is as radical and challenging in our own time as it was in the days when Jesus washed feet in Jerusalem and Paul wrote letters to the youthful Christian communities. Along with the other images we have looked at, it inspires our allegiance and fidelity to the new creation in Christ. We turn now to see how these images come together in the vocation of a minister to lead the people of God to the destination of their hearts.

A Vocation of Leadership

Taking up a vocation can be described in the language of a journey. It is a quest, a turning away from some previous destination toward a new one, or perhaps the discovery of a destination at a time when you had none, lost in a dark wood. Luke's description of the conversion of Paul has him starting out on one journey and ending up on quite another, and Paul himself is careful to record his movements after his calling, tracking the first of his many pilgrimages of faith.

Linda's journey began when she was drawn to the ministry by the image of the priest. She will discover that following the image will lead her into a deeper awareness of other images as well. She may find herself called to preach a gospel that challenges many of the teachings of the church. She may find herself called to pastor people who will reject her authority, and she may find herself called to serve a church while she questions whether that church truly serves God. She may find that the priest who mediates God and humanity stands on the edge in a spot that seems lonely and crowded at the same time.

What Linda will discover is that none of the images of a minister can be followed in isolation. Anyone trying to answer "Whose story do I tell?" at once encounters the answers given to that question over many centuries, and the answers being given in many communities today. The same is true of the questions asked by the other images. In fact, as I suggested in chapter 1, those questions themselves arise from the attempt to lead people to the destination of their hearts, to be the kind of ministers who embody the story of Jesus in a way that increases the love of God and neighbor. The questions and their possible answers come from the sharp juxtaposition of the story of what is going on now with the story of Christ that gives direction and purpose to restless hearts. The images we have looked at shape ministers not toward private ends but for leadership in the Body of Christ, where "if one part is hurt, all the parts share its pain. And if one part is honoured, all the parts share its joy" (I Cor. 12:26).

In the shifting interaction of these images, we may find some comfort from Paul. "I accommodated myself to people in all kinds of different situations, so that by all possible means I might bring some to salvation. All this I do for the sake of the gospel, that I might share its benefits with others" (I Cor.

9:22-23). Rather than resting secure in one image, the call to enable the Body of Christ to change requires the minister to adopt many images. Sometimes moral leadership requires the exhortation of the preacher. Keeping the destination in sight may require the critical reflection of the teacher. Keeping the Body together and caring for the parts in pain may require the ministrations of the pastor. Strengthening the Body for the journey and making bridges into new lands may require the mediation of the priest. And keeping the movement aimed at love, that best way of all, may require the forceful humility of the servant. All these images work together in the vocation of this minister to lead the people of God.

The call to ministry leads those who respond into a vocation of leadership and sets them forth on a journey lived out on the edge. As we pursue this journey we will encounter situations where passivity seems preferable to leadership, where the temptation not to lead and the temptation to betray seem more reasonable than the journey undertaken when we tell the story of the God revealed in Christ. We may wonder why we answered the call in the first place, when it leaves us watching well-cappings, answering midnight phone calls, attending fractious church meetings, and torn by complex allegiances. It may seem that the only image uniting those we have explored is that of the fool for Christ's sake. If that is so, at least we have Paul's assurance that it is perfectly normal and nothing to be wondered at. "God chose those who by human standards are fools to shame the wise" (I Cor. 1:27). Paul's words must not be taken as a justification for deliberate ignorance or as compensation for constant failure as a minister, because, as Paul continues, such a choice of fools is made instead "so that no human being might feel boastful before God" (I Cor. 1:29). Perhaps we might discover with Paul that only fools for Christ are sufficiently wise to become moral leaders of God's people. In that case, such foolishness will be wisdom enough for the task.

CHAPTER 3

TRANSFORMING MINISTRY

The apostle Paul had the knack many good leaders seem to have for remembering that communities are made up of individuals. Of course, he knew there are corporate dimensions to community life. He was capable of writing letters, originally addressed to small church groups, whose significance to the church at large became apparent in his own lifetime. Yet even in his most doctrinal letters, he never forgets the names and faces who make up "the church" to which he writes. Toward the end of his letter to the Romans, Paul greets or commends twenty-nine women and men and five households by name or personal reference and mentions eight names besides himself in his farewell. It is a practice characteristic of his ministry.

Yet such references do not simply reveal Paul's gregarious nature or his penchant for personal appeals. They also reveal much about the diversity of ministry in the early church and the setting of that ministry in a particular historical and cultural context. "My greetings to Prisca and Aquila, my fellow-workers in Christ Jesus, who risked their own necks to save my life; to them, thanks not only from me, but from all the churches among the gentiles; and my greetings to the church at their house" (Rom. 16:3-5a).

Paul's itinerant ministry was connected with regional communities and house churches. He acknowledged his reliance on his co-workers, in this case a woman and a man in shared leadership, and points out their bravery and solidarity in the service of the gospel. All this is put in the setting of a community of prayer and worship meeting in their own home.[1]

Prisca, Aquila, and Paul experienced a personal call to a public ministry in the first recorded generation of the Christian church. It was a call they heard and answered in the company of co-workers, household communities, and widely scattered churches, a call constrained and shaped by the freedom of the gospel and the limits of Hellenistic culture. We have looked at some important features of how the call to ministry is heard. Now we will look at some features of the social setting in which response to the call takes place, at the relationship between leaders and followers as ministers take up their vocation of leadership, and at the possibility of that leadership's continually transforming leaders and followers toward the increase of the love of God and neighbor.

The Setting of Ministry

In the earliest of Paul's surviving letters,[2] he gives us an important glimpse into one of the social dilemmas of ministry. "You remember, brothers, with what unsparing energy we used to work, slaving night and day so as not to be a burden on any one of you while we were proclaiming the gospel of God to you." (I Thess. 2:9). Paul was convinced that no one should be paid for preaching the gospel. This set him apart from other religious figures of his day, some of whom expected to receive goods and services, if not outright remuneration, in return for their spiritual efforts on behalf of local communities.[3] He may not have been able to maintain this ideal. Paul thanks the Philippians at length for supporting his ministry (Phil. 4:14-20) and writes ahead asking Philemon to prepare lodging should he be able to come to him (Philem. 22). In fact, Paul wants to have it both ways. He asks the Corinthians, "What soldier would ever serve in the army at his own expense?" (I Cor. 9:7) and quotes the law of Moses, "You must not muzzle an ox when it is treading out the corn" (I Cor. 9:9). Going further, he recalls "The Lord gave the instruction that those who preach the gospel should get their living from the gospel" (I Cor. 9:14). Yet he maintains that "in my preaching I offer the gospel free of charge to avoid using the rights which the gospel allows me" (I Cor. 9:18).

Paul has his practiced tentmaker's finger on a delicate problem. He knew that preaching the gospel was a full-time vocation requiring great personal sacrifice and expense. He knew that there was precedent both in Jewish custom and early Christian tradition for those who sowed spiritually to reap materially. Yet he also knew the resentments that might build if he demanded the support that was his by right, and I suspect he would have grasped at once the latter-day saying that the one who pays the piper calls the tune. In a typically ironic fashion, he avoids the rights the gospel gives him in order to free the gospel from human bondage.

However well Paul may have dealt with the problem, the model of the self-sustaining minister who does not depend on others for support is not part of the social setting of most vocations of ministry today. And with the acceptance of support come constraints on the gospel a minister seeks to serve. In the stories we have looked at earlier, the minister watching the well-capping realizes that if he opposes it, he may very well lose his job. The minister trying to hush the woman with a marital problem may tell himself his job description does not cover marriage counseling, because he is reluctant to engage issues that would upset his parishioners. The young minister told not to give public aid to AIDS workers realizes that if she opposes her pastor her own career may well suffer and with it her ability to help others in the future. The associate facing a divided social concerns committee realizes that some of those people either literally or figuratively sign her paycheck.

We can get a sense of some of the problems posed by the social setting of ministry by considering what Linda encountered once she decided to respond to her call. Linda entered seminary to explore her call and receive training for her vocation to the ministry. She had not yet settled on a church in which to seek ordination and appointment, because of the barriers to women's ordination placed by the Baptist and Catholic churches she had known. Although she is visiting an Episcopal church as she begins her studies at a Methodist seminary, she has not yet made a commitment to a church, nor has one officially chosen her. As a result, she has no institutional support for attending seminary. On the one hand, this gives her freedom in where to go and what to take as she explores her call. On the other hand, it puts the financial burden of attending school directly on her and delays her introduction into the polity and placement procedures of an actual communion in which she might someday serve.

Linda finds she must continue working as a free-lance accountant to help pay for her theological education. That gives her considerably less time and energy for seminary than she would otherwise have. She finds that many of her fellow students also work, most of them at part-time church jobs that not only help in financing their education but also give them valuable professional experience, along with a foot in the door of the institutional church. The more she learns about both the Episcopal and the Methodist churches, the more she finds that there are career ladders in them just as there were in the accounting firm she left. She begins to feel pressured to choose a church in order to get on the ladder while still in seminary. She also realizes that her theological exploration cannot be as free as she had hoped, for her course work will be shaped just as much by the vision of the church she enters regarding the proper preparation for ministry as by her interests and needs.

Linda begins to sense a change in the way her family and friends regard her. Once they accepted that her new beginning was not just a temporary aberration, they had to see her not as a rising business professional but as a prospective minister. This puzzled them. They did not have many role models for what a woman minister is supposed to be like. Her friends from the accounting firm asked her whether the Lord had a comprehensive dental plan. Other friends her own age became embarrassed to tell certain jokes around her. When she visited her old home, her parents remarked that if she wanted to do ministry she might be more comfortable visiting the sick than preaching. The people from her Catholic prayer group were proud of her and made her feel like a pioneer, whereas many of her fellow students kept asking her what she was going to do with her education if she didn't have a place to work. As the year went on, her sense of a call to ministry continued to deepen, but she began to worry more and more about how to turn her vocation into something she could actually do.

Hearing the call may be personal, but responding to it plunges Linda into a complex social setting. She is discovering that her vocation is also a job, a profession, and a career. As a job it is work she does in exchange for food, clothing, shelter, and money. As a profession it is defined by cultural roles and expectations that she has little choice about and that she might find herself fighting against. As a career it makes her desire to minister subject to the judgments of others and makes her personal style of ministry dependent on her conforming to standards defined by the church.[4]

What Linda is discovering, in the terms we spoke of in chapter 1, is that the social setting of the vocation of ministry tends to pull ministers toward the center of their communities rather than toward the edge. As Paul knew well, when ministers are employees, those who pay them define their tasks. When ministry is a traditional profession, the cumulative weight of roles and expectations functions to control the character and activity of the minister. When the minister must balance conscience and career, the interests of the status quo often make a powerful alliance with the interests of a career. It is easier for the minister to follow the center's desire for stability and continuity than to hear the edge's call for vitality and change.

If Linda graduates, is ordained, and receives an appointment to a church, she will discover there are many other constraints on her vocation on the other side of seminary. She will find the center pulling not just on her and the institutional church but on the lives of her parishioners as well. She will find ministers and laypeople torn between reaching out to others and taking care of themselves. Where Paul ran into legalists and libertines, she is more likely to encounter racism, sexism, and nationalism. Where Paul fought the idolatry of pagan worship, she may find herself fighting the idolatries of money and violence. She will discover all this and more as she pursues her vocation of leading people to God. In order to understand the challenges Linda and all of us will face in trying to exercise moral leadership, we need now to look more closely at the relationship between leaders and followers.

Leaders and Followers

Earlier we saw that leadership has to do with the movement of people through time and change. The possibility of movement arises from the consciousness of conflict, as the stories people had used to understand themselves and the world begin to fail under stress. We saw that leaders who live on the edge of a community rather than in its center are more likely to become aware of the sort of conflict that generates movement. Leaders on the edge are also more likely to be aware of the conflicting stories that contend for the hearts of their communities and to be open to fresh interpretations of the stories that call people onward in life.

The associate minister at the social concerns meeting, newly arrived and not yet established in the center of the community, can see what the competing parties may not be able to recognize. She can see at least three important stories at work. One group is clearly guided by a story that gives priority to the defense of traditional American values and Christian family life and that therefore opposes abortion as murder committed by deviant individuals but supports capital punishment as killing justified by society as a whole. Another group has clearly been shaped by a story that gives priority to the defense of all life and that therefore makes a connection between opposing abortion and opposing capital punishment, because they both require the taking of life. The associate minister also sees, but more dimly, the story of that church congregation at work, as it has shaped over a long period of time what issues are important to the community and how disputes have been handled. What she cannot see even dimly, as the shouting continues, is how the larger Christian story is present. Both sides feel God is on their side. Her challenge as a leader is to discern how the Christian story has been told in that community and how to bring it to bear in a fresh and critical manner on the divisive issues at hand.[5]

Imagine the following scene. A long-time member of an old downtown church has died, leaving a sizable legacy to the church with the stipulation that it be used for restoration or new construction on the physical plant. The pastor and senior lay members have conducted a series of meetings gathering information about what options the church has for using the money and what the desires of the church members might be. Three options emerge, each with supporters in the church. One group suggests the money be used for extensive repairs to the infrastructure of the entire physical plant, including the parsonage, since roofing, plumbing, painting, and electrical needs have suffered neglect over the years. Another group wants to use the money to convert a seldom used church-school building into a modern community center with a small gymnasium and a fully equipped media center. A third group sees this gift as the chance to replace some of the stained-glass windows in the main church building and to purchase a larger organ, which would require substantial renovation of the choir loft as well.

At an open meeting the groups make their reports to the church, and the pastor makes the following observations. The amount of the gift will only allow one of the projects to be completed, in their present forms. The projects seem to have strong backing by particular groups, but everyone agrees that all three are worth doing. The pastor recalls that over the years the church has been a close-knit community and has always taken the needs of different groups in the church very seriously. Indeed, the main reason the physical plant has not been kept in better repair has been the unwillingness of the church to divert funds away from its youth ministries and senior citizens' programs. The pastor suggests that renovating the church-school building for a community center would help restore part of the physical plant and might even help in attracting more youth and young adults to the church's graying membership. Yet those aims could be met without the somewhat elaborate plans drawn up for that renovation. A more modest community center would leave funds for at least partial work on other painting and electrical projects and would likely be enough to clean, though not replace, the stained glass. The church could live with the old plumbing, roof, and organ for now, and plan their restoration as the opportunity arose.

Combining the projects this way might help revitalize the church and would accomplish some of what each group would like to see happen. The pastor's remarks met with general acceptance by the first two groups, and after a while the third group joined in, although letting it be known that they hope this will mean that a new organ and choir loft will take priority over further restoration in the future.

The pastor, with the assistance of other church members, took steps to draw out the community's desires and assisted in focusing them into concrete plans. The pastor then acted as a broker of the desires represented by those plans, being sensitive to the needs of each group, putting the process in the context of the congregation's past story and suggesting a fourth option that would extend their history of cooperation and compromise. The third group "got" less than the other two, but the pastor was able to help them see this as something positive for the community, which was no doubt made easier by agreeing to give their plans first priority when the occasion arose.

As a leader, the pastor enabled the transaction of desires among the groups, appealing to their common story and allowing them to exchange parts of their plans for the good of the whole community. The pastor acted within the common story, helping to get things done in a way that would further strengthen it while relying on, rather than questioning, its basic assumptions and values. We could say that the pastor operated mostly in the center of the community, though with enough angle of vision to see a fourth option that combined the other three. We could also say that the overall purpose of this transaction was set by the three groups within the church that formulated the original plans, with the pastor coming in to guide the process in a helpful way. The deeper story of the church as a Christian community was not part of the transaction. Leaders and followers were bound together out of mutual interest, but their allegiance to the ultimate grounds of that story in Christ was not directly addressed. Nonetheless, a beneficial transaction occurred within the community, where members cooperated openly and maintained a sense of continuity with their past.[6]

But suppose things had gone another way. Suppose the bequest had been handled by a lawyer who was a prominent member of the church. He goes to the pastor with the good news and does not make a public announcement. The pastor responds by getting together a small group of the more powerful members of the church and laying the opportunity before them. This group decides what it wants to do with the money and then agrees to "sell" this plan to the community at large by presenting it as the only choice available. They thank the pastor for "keeping things under his hat."

Or suppose the pastor, upon discovering the bequest, realizes that this is his chance to fulfill a long-standing dream to purchase audio-video equipment for local broadcasting of the Sunday morning services. He knows that when word gets out, there will be a difference of opinion in the church on how to use the money. He also knows that the chairperson of the finance committee has wanted a new organ and choir loft for a long time. The pastor goes to the chairperson, who goes to other members of the committee, and one thing leads to another. Later, when the bequest becomes public, several proposals are made for the use of the money. When the church board puts the matter up for a vote, the project that is approved provides for a new choir loft, an organ, and audio-video equipment.

These are not scenes of community transaction but of the manipulative wielding of power. Both scenes are characterized by a coalition of special interests acting without regard for the interests of less powerful members of the community. Both require the manipulation of others to gain the ends sought by the power-wielders. In the first case, it does not even matter what the small group's plan is, because whatever it is it's the only plan allowed to form. In the second case, the pastor allies himself with someone in a position to get what he wants done. Although other proposals may be allowed to surface, it is only for appearances' sake, because the outcome has been arranged beforehand.

Power, the ability to get things done, has served the purposes of those who have it, and the process has robbed other members of the community of the chance to participate in the decision on the bequest. The pastor gains in both cases, but differently. In the first he gains the approval of significant people in the community and puts them in his debt. In the second he also gains a new medium for building his own power base outside the home congregation.

The relation between leaders and followers that occurs in either case is not really transactional, for there was no open brokering of interests widely representative of the community, only the advancing of a few individuals and their private aims. There was also no appeal to the common story of the community, let alone to the larger Christian story itself. It is even hard to say that the power-wielders—the pastor and other church board members who "managed" the bequest—worked in the center of the community, for their private manipulation left them in no greater solidarity with the center of the community than with the edge. It would be more accurate to say that the power-wielders took *themselves* to be the center. Such a situation is a grave threat to the life of the community, for it not only makes the center arbitrary and secretive but leaves it only as stable as the temporary alliance of interests that brought the power-wielders to act in concert.[7]

But suppose things went differently still. Suppose that word got out from the start and that only two groups had formed within the church around plans for using the legacy. One group wished to turn the old church-school building into a community center and to put in three small offices that the church would lease for a dollar a year to neighborhood activist groups. They had letters of interest from people involved in child care, prison ministries, outreach to persons with AIDS, night shelters, drug rehabilitation, and ministry to unwed mothers. This group felt the church had been isolated from its urban neighbors for too long and wanted to use the legacy to make amends and become a vital part of the community.

Another group strongly disagreed. They were scandalized at how the main church building had been left to deteriorate and felt its unattractive appearance was an offense to the memory of past members as well as an obstacle to the recruitment of new ones. They wanted to use the money to refurnish the main church building completely, including a new roof, repairs to plaster, new stained glass, new paint, new pews, and a new organ and choir loft. They were sharply opposed to the first group, feeling that social outreach had to come second after taking care of the church community, especially since the money had come from a third-generation church member. The open meeting called by the pastor ended in a disastrous shouting match with no resolution.

This profoundly troubled the pastor, who was shocked to learn of the deep divisions in the church that only surfaced when this unexpected money made it possible to plan for real changes. This incident seemed to call into question the church's very reasons for being, as it revealed two different congregations in the same building. Could the church survive this sort of struggle?

Transactional leadership would not work here. The groups were too deeply divided to see that each could benefit from some third option. Each thought there was something morally wrong about the other's plans. The pastor could not broker interests when neither side was prepared to bargain. Power-wielding would certainly be a temptation, but it would be difficult to pull off. Even if a small group of power-wielders could agree on a course of action, there were powerful church members on each side of the split. Trying to manipulate them would almost surely result in the splintering of the church.

The pastor could not appeal successfully to the common story of the church's past, for the dispute over the legacy revealed undercurrents of dissent in that very story. Each group offered conflicting interpretations of the past, with correspondingly different assessments of how to carry that story into the future. The pastor could not appeal directly to the larger Christian story, for the split in the church revealed two very different ways that story seemed to be operating in the congregation. Any appeal to the past or vision of a possible future would require a new telling of the church's story *and* the Christian story, in the midst of what amounted to a fundamental crisis in the identity of the congregation.

The pastor realized that he could not lead without a destination, and he was not going to get one from the divided church. He had to resolve in his own heart what kind of people the church was called to be and then find some way to make that vision available to the rest of the church. He had to transform his own understanding and assist in the transformation of others. This was a difficult and risky business, for it was impossible to foretell the results of such transformation. He understood and respected the position of both groups. But he felt that the church had to be loyal to a larger story than its own history and needed to do more than simply make amends for years of indifference to church structures *or* the world outside the church's walls. The church needed a transformation in its understanding of what it meant to *be* a Christian church in its present historical circumstances. The pastor became more and more aware that any forceful response he might make would push him closer to the edge of the community. Yet he also realized that the only way he could lead in this situation was from some new angle that would transform the vision of all concerned.

The pastor was experiencing the birth in conflict of the possibility of transforming leadership.[8] Such leadership changes leaders and followers, because it asks them both to hear their own story differently, to hear new stories that challenge their self-understanding, and to be willing to change in the interests of a transformed vision of where the destination of their hearts would lead them to go. It requires leaders to take a stand based on conviction rather than pragmatism or self-interest and to risk their leadership in trying to awaken those convictions in others. It requires followers to become critical of their own understanding of their needs and interests. It requires leaders and followers alike to take unconventional steps to resolve issues their conventional stories cannot comprehend.

Transforming leadership requires that leaders help followers articulate their deepest moral goals and reshape their lives to bring about real and intended social change toward those goals. In the chapters to come, we will see that ministers like the pastor of the church with a legacy may spend most of their time in transactional leadership. They will no doubt be tempted to power-wielding, especially in the face of the sort of conflict that calls for the riskier path of transformation. We will see that the minister as moral leader helps the people of God to become aware of the stories that have been guiding them and offers a new telling of the story of God revealed in Christ that will best help them embody the vision of the good that story offers to their hearts. Before going on, however, we must look at how the vocation of the Christian minister makes taking up the challenge of a transforming ministry both necessary and possible in this uncertain world.

The Possibility of Transformation

Paul's picture of the life of a Christian leader would scarcely have much appeal as a job description today.

> To this day, we go short of food and drink and clothes, we are beaten up and we have no homes; we earn our living by labouring with our own hands; when we are cursed, we answer with a blessing; when we are hounded, we endure it passively; when we are insulted, we give a courteous answer. We are treated even now as the dregs of the world, the very lowest scum. (I Cor. 4:11-13)

I think I can be forgiven for finding it implausible that Paul *always* gave a courteous answer! But it must be admitted that he does not paint a very attractive portrait of the life of the apostle. He does so, he says, "so there is to be no boasting about human beings" (I Cor. 3:21). Later, in correspondence to those same Corinthians, he gives some indication of why he is willing to be a fool for Christ, why he perseveres through such awful opposition, why his entire way of judging the world and what happens to him in it has been transformed.

> From now onwards, then, we will not consider anyone by human standards: even if we were once familiar with Christ by human standards, we do not know him in that way any longer. So for anyone who is in Christ, there is a new creation: the old order is gone and a new being is there to see. It is all God's work; he

59

> reconciled us to himself through Christ and he gave us the ministry of reconciliation. I mean, God was in Christ reconciling the world to himself, not holding anyone's faults against them, but entrusting to us the message of reconciliation.   (II Cor. 5:16-19)

The Christian life begins in transformation. That is sometimes a hard message for contemporary Christians to hear. What was a religion of conversion has become for many an accident of history, not something that irrupts into our lives but a condition we were born into along with our parents' social class and political affiliation. That is not, of course, true for everyone, as the widespread growth of born-again congregations shows. But even there one wonders how fully chosen Christianity is, how radical the transformation, how "new" the new creation, for the world on the other side of rebirth seems familiar, controlled, predictable.

In fact, the real reason the message of transformation is hard to hear is that it asks us to be subject to constant change. It tells us that however the world once was, we can count on the new world to be different. However we once judged others and ourselves, we must adopt a new standard, that of Christ, for the future. And we must do this in the service of a story that gives us precious little concrete guidance on how to live this new creation and lead others to live there as well. We find instead a whirling mix of Jewish traditions and Hellenistic morals and Galilean parables and stories of Jesus, which sometimes cohere and often conflict. Even if we could come to some agreement on the moral teachings we do find in the Scriptures of the Christian story, we would be hard put to find explicit answers to the hard questions surrounding AIDS, nuclear war, reproductive technology, and other conundrums of the modern age. All we are assured of is that somehow we are new, and in trying to figure out what that means, Paul tells us, "Do not model your behaviour on the contemporary world, but let the renewing of your minds transform you, so that you may discern for yourselves what is the will of God—what is good and acceptable and mature" (Rom. 12:2).

Such transformation is both a mandate and a challenge for the minister as moral leader. We saw earlier that as Linda moves into the social setting of ministry, she finds her personal vocation becoming a public profession, defined and shaped by the institutional church whose offices of leadership she will one day try to fill. Yet the moral authority for leadership lies in the larger story of the Christian people, not in the offices its communities establish. Since the authority for the office lies in the story that forms the community, those who inhabit the offices are accountable to the story and to the community. Their leadership is open to challenge through the reinterpretation of the story by members of the community. Followers also are subject to the authority of the story. They too must refuse to conform and must let their minds be transformed.

Ministry must be transforming, and for that to happen we must be continually transforming ministry. In some dark times during the struggle for civil rights, Martin Luther King, Jr., preached a sermon on the text from Romans just quoted above. He called it the "Transformed Nonconformist," and he aimed Paul's remark at ministers, at the institutional church, and at the members of Christian congregations. He urged a return to the nonconformity of the early Christians, transformed by the gospel to judge themselves and the world by a new standard. And he warned of the dire consequences of failure in this effort at transforming the ministry of all Christians.

> This hour in history needs a dedicated circle of transformed nonconformists. Our planet teeters on the brink of atomic annihilation; dangerous passions of pride, hatred, and selfishness are enthroned in our lives; truth lies prostrate on the rugged hills of nameless calvaries; and men do reverence before false gods of nationalism and materialism. The saving of our world from pending doom will come, not through the complacent adjustment of the conforming majority, but through the creative maladjustment of a nonconforming minority.[9]

The continual transformation of leaders and followers, which is nothing more than the transforming ministry of all Christians in the new creation, means that leaders and followers are often out of step. The greater the degree of transformation called for by "renewed minds," the greater degree of tension between such leaders and those they would lead, the greater the distance from the edge to the center of the community. This is the sort of tension that caused Paul to describe the lot of the apostle in such harsh terms, but it is the same tension that moved him to bemoan the "stupid people" in Galatia who allowed themselves to be misled by a false telling of the Christian story. It is only by telling and retelling that story anew that the tension between leaders and followers can be resolved in movement toward our common destination in Christ.

The constant push against the standards of the world makes transactional leadership necessary but not sufficient for the minister as moral leader. Sooner or later, every leader will find that the "old order" fails in the face of contemporary challenges, that no amount of brokering will substitute for a transforming breakthrough into the new creation. And every breakthrough itself will be only temporary. One generation's answer will become the stumbling block for the next. As Paul said, "It is not being circumcised or uncircumcised that matters, but what matters is a new creation" (Gal. 6:15). Our movement into that new creation may be uncertain, but it is certainly fueled by the stories of the people of God over the centuries in which they have made their unending pilgrimage of faith, and in those stories we can find bread for the journey today.

Continual transformation is required to keep the people of God moving toward the destination of their hearts. Transforming ministry in the leadership of that movement is a difficult and threatening enterprise in an uncertain world and in the face of such wide rifts in the Body of Christ. Yet taking up that leadership as a vocation and trusting in our ability in Christ to live it out is, as Paul would put it, another way of boasting not in humans but in the Lord. Moral leadership is a daunting prospect for the minister, perhaps even more fearsome than shipwrecks or scourgings. It is perhaps less of a threat and more of a challenge if we remember that the church is neither the world nor the reign of God, but something suspended between them, whose relative movement we can and must affect as those called by God to love.

CHAPTER 4

THE MINISTER AS MORAL LEADER

There is an account, perhaps apocryphal, of an interview with a famous Southern writer, who was asked, "Why do you Southerners tell such bizarre and outlandish stories?" The author replied, "Because if we told the truth, no one would believe us." The point, of course, is highly ironic. Telling the truth about things people would rather not believe requires the telling of stories. The Polish author Stanislaw Lem puts these words in the mouth of a storyteller called to perform before a powerful and capricious king:

> "O King!" answered Trurl. "You would learn from me what is perfection and how it may be gained, yet prove unable to grasp the deep meanings and great truths with which my narratives abound. Truly, you seek amusement and not wisdom—yet, even as you listen, my words do slowly penetrate and act upon your brain, and later too will act, much as a time bomb."[1]

Stories entertaining and diverting, yet dangerously compelling, abound in Christian tradition as well. The parables of Jesus used the elements of everyday storytelling, but those who had ears to hear found them enlightening and disturbing. Two great leaders of the Christian church—Antony, one of the founders of monasticism, and Augustine, one of the architects of Western Christianity—were transformed by stories that carried truths too powerful to ignore. Augustine spent years on a quest for spiritual truth, but he tells us his heart found its destination nearer when he heard stories of other conversions and knew such a resting place was a real possibility for people like himself. One of the stories he heard was that of Antony, who himself had found a new destination after hearing the story of the rich young ruler. Augustine found that it spoke directly to him, as perhaps our minister watching the well-capping does today in recalling the story of the good Samaritan.[2]

Leaders hear powerful stories and tell them to those they would lead. In the process they find inspiration for their own leadership and offer destinations to people of restless hearts. From the pivotal days of the Montgomery bus boycott, Martin Luther King, Jr., told this story in a sermon, "Our God Is Able."

> After a particularly strenuous day, I settled in bed at a late hour. My wife had already fallen asleep and I was about to doze off when the telephone rang. An angry voice said, "Listen, nigger, we've taken all we want from you. Before next week you'll be sorry you ever came to Montgomery." I hung up, but I could not sleep. It seemed that all of my fears had come down on me at once. I had reached the saturation point.
>
> I got out of bed and began to walk the floor. Finally, I went to the kitchen and heated a pot of coffee. I was ready to give up. I tried to think of a way to move out of the picture without appearing to be a coward. In this state of exhaustion, when my courage had almost gone, I determined to take my problem to God. My head in my hands, I bowed over the kitchen table and prayed aloud. The words I spoke to God that midnight are still vivid in my memory. "I am here taking a stand for what I believe is right. But now I am afraid. The people are looking to me for leadership, and if I stand before them without strength and courage, they too will falter. I am at the end of my powers. I have nothing left. I've come to the point where I can't face it alone."
>
> At that moment I experienced the presence of the Divine as I had never before experienced him. It seemed as though I could hear the quiet assurance of an inner voice, saying, "Stand up for righteousness, stand up for truth. God will be at your side forever." Almost at once my fears began to pass from me. My uncertainty disappeared. I was ready to face anything. The outer situation remained the same, but God had given me inner calm.[3]

King's story shows a leader in a situation where the consciousness of conflict has given rise to the possibility of movement, but where the direction of that movement is so frightening, the journey to the destination so arduous, that even the leader is tempted to turn back. At the moment of crisis, the leader draws on a tradition of prayer and tells his story to God, finding strength in God's reply and courage in the assurance of God's presence. The story of that experience then itself becomes part of the process of leadership, as King recasts his personal story in his public sermon, making it accessible to others in bolstering their own faith and courage in a time of trial.[4]

King would not have been able to tell his story to God had he not had the language of prayer available to him, a language he received with the telling of the Christian story in the community of faith. He would not have been able to hear the words of assurance in a time of fear had he not heard stories of God assuring others before him, for he had heard the words of Yahweh to another leader, Joshua: "Have I not told you: Be strong and stand firm? Be fearless and undaunted, for go where you may, Yahweh your God is with you" (Josh. 1:9), and the closing words of Matthew, "And look, I am with you always; yes, to the end of time." (Matt. 28:20).[5] He would not have been able to use his story in the exercise of leadership had there not existed practices of storytelling in preaching that enabled him to introduce his account by saying, "As I come to the conclusion of my message, I would wish you to permit a personal experience."[6]

King may have preached that God is able, but it was the leadership of other people before him in the Body of Christ that enabled King to lead as he did, for they kept alive the story that gave him a compelling destination and the courage to keep striding toward it. In looking at how the minister as moral leader tells the Christian story so that others may live it and tell it in turn, we will be helped by imagining where the story is told and what difference this makes for those who tell and those who hear. We will look at *telling the story in the center, telling the story on the edge,* and the dangerous opportunities in *hearing new voices and telling new stories.*

Telling the Story in the Center

Paul closes I Corinthians with some rather specific instructions.

> Now about the collection for God's holy people; you are to do the same as I prescribed for the churches in Galatia. On the first day of the week, each of you should put aside and reserve as much as each of you can spare; do not delay the collection until I arrive. When I come, I will send to Jerusalem with letters of introduction those people you approve to deliver your gift; if it is worth my going too, they can travel with me. (I Cor. 16:1-4)

Paul was directing the Corinthians to play their part in sending assistance to the poor Christians of Jerusalem. He had apparently participated in a similar collection from the church at Antioch early in his career (Acts 11:27-30). Now, with the help of Titus and others (II Cor. 8:1-24), he was organizing a large collection from the Gentile churches (Rom. 15:25-29; II Cor. 9:1-5) that would demonstrate in concrete terms the solidarity of Paul's mission with the Jewish Christians in Jerusalem (Gal. 2:10; Acts 24:17).

But Paul's straightforward directive may not have worked, for we find him appealing to the Corinthians again in very different terms in II Corinthians 8 and 9. His first appeal had all the hallmarks of the confident use of power and authority. "You know about the collection; well, then do as I've told everybody else to do and contribute. Here's how and when." Paul assumes his power as he assumes the Corinthians' obedience. He makes no attempt to put the collection in a framework consistent with the story of Christ he has brought them. He makes no appeal to individuals or to groups within the community, and no appeal to shared motives and interests with other Christian groups. It is as if he speaks not in the center of the community nor from its edge but somehow detached from it altogether.

How differently he begins in II Corinthians 8!

> Next, brothers, we will tell you of the grace of God which has been granted to the churches of Macedonia, and how, throughout continual ordeals of hardship, their unfailing joy

and their intense poverty have overflowed in a wealth of generosity on their part. I can testify that it was of their own accord that they made their gift, which was not merely as far as their resources would allow, but well beyond their resources; and they had kept imploring us most insistently for the privilege of a share in the fellowship of service to God's holy people. (II Cor. 8:1-4)

Paul goes beyond holding up the example of these fellow Christians. He points out that the Corinthians had already started on this project, working with Titus, and can now bring it to a successful conclusion (II Cor. 8:6, 10-11). He praises the Corinthians for the richness of their faith and urges them to excel in giving as well (II Cor. 8:7). He backs off his earlier stark directive by remarking, "I am not saying this as an order, but testing the genuineness of your love against the concern of others" (II Cor. 8:8). Despite noting that the Macedonians had given out of their poverty, he gives the Corinthians some leeway by saying that they don't have to give to the point of hardship and suggests some benefit in reciprocal generosity when he says, "Your surplus at present may fill their deficit, and another time their surplus may fill your deficit" (II Cor. 8:14). He assures them they need have no fears about his management of the contribution and identifies individuals responsible for it (II Cor. 8:16-24). But most persuasively of all, perhaps, Paul sets the act of giving in the context of the story of Christ: "You are well aware of the generosity which our Lord Jesus Christ had, that, although he was rich, he became poor for your sake, so that you should become rich through his poverty" (II Cor. 8:9).[7]

Here Paul is telling the story in the center of the Corinthian community. He is not telling it *from* that center but *in* it. He stands on the edge of it, not simply in writing from afar but also because he represents communities in Macedonia and Jerusalem as well. Yet he is drawing on local structures of community and their history. He is attentive to the resources and motives present in the community. He both praises and challenges the Corinthians, managing to confront them while communicating concern for their interests and accomplishments. He acknowledges their perspective but insists that the story that shapes their community also connects them with other communities and does so in a way that models generous sharing.

In II Corinthians 9, a passage probably drawn from other correspondence but attached here,[8] Paul quotes the stories of the people of God to support his appeal, noting that "God loves a cheerful giver" and that "to the needy he gave without stint, his uprightness stands firm forever" (II Cor. 9:7-9, echoing Prov. 22:8 and Ps. 112:9). He closes by emphasizing that not only will other communities feel bound in fellowship through their fellow Christians' generosity, but praise will also be given to God for the grace evident in the gift. "At the same time, their prayer for you will express the affection they feel for you because of the unbounded grace God has given you. Thanks be to God for his gift that is beyond all telling!" (II Cor. 9:14-15).

We do not know how well the Corinthians responded, but it is easy to imagine a better response from Paul's second appeal than from his first! It might have been the original stewardship campaign, a combination of praise, cajolery, and sincere yet shrewd appeals to the heart of the Christian story. Knowing the community involved, brokering its interests, relying on resident structures of authority and decision making, making direct appeals to the acknowledged story calling the community into being—these are the hallmarks of a leader telling the story in the center.[9]

The same traits are visible in the first resolution to the story of the legacy we considered in chapter 3. The pastor called on well-established members of the community to help shape a broad consensus on what to do with the legacy. He worked through existing networks of relationship, tapping the various power bases within the community in doing so, while keeping the process public and letting everyone have his or her say. He kept himself apart from the three proposals that emerged, preserving his ability to broker each group's interests with integrity. He had obviously learned the peculiar accidents of history that had shaped the community's own story and had a pretty good idea of what sort of proposal would allow it to move forward in continuity not just with its past story but with the larger Christian story it professed.

His proposal appealed to the vested interests of each group, but more so to their common sense of a shared destination in what kind of people they felt called to become as a church. In doing this he took on the images of pastor, priest, and servant, exercising care, mediating, and enabling the different groups to see themselves as one. He was telling the story in the center of the community, helping to clarify how it would respond in a way that would truthfully represent the character of the community.

Yet *telling* the story in the center does not mean *living* in the center of the community. The associate minister at the social concerns committee meeting might respond by telling the story in the center even though she was not yet "established." She was relatively ignorant of the history of the community, unconnected with its powerful members, and carried the additional burden of their suspicion of her as a woman in ministry. When the meeting erupted in bitter disagreement, she had little knowledge of what long-term interests were at stake, let alone what proposal might represent a prudent brokering of the parties involved. Now she may well have to extend herself into the realm of the more transforming leadership (to be looked at below) in order to resolve the particular issues raised. But the fact that her church has a social concerns committee at all and that she participates in its deliberations is part of the ongoing moral discourse in the community, and it is this discourse that must first be maintained by her telling the story in the center.

She can do this by calling the character of the community into question. She can raise the question of whether the story of Christ is operating in the way the community is interacting at this moment. She could ask, "Is *this* how we talk to each other in this church? Is this how we express our Christian concern?" That may appear as if she is only appealing to good manners, and in a way she is. But much more than that, she is living out the image of the teacher, asking whose truth is present in the meeting. She gives the people a chance to see themselves reflected in someone else's eyes and to hear her asking them if this is indeed the sort of behavior both the story of that church's past and the larger story of Christ would have them exhibit. Her appeal may fall on deaf ears in the heat of the moment. But it shows her to be solidly among them, willing to risk their displeasure by speaking in what is after all a rather blunt and accusing fashion, if one wanted to take it that way.

In doing so she is also performing her vocational task of asking the simple and quite dangerous question of what Christ has to do with all this. She may not at this stage transform anyone's perspective enough to resolve the divisive issues. But she may be able to lay the groundwork for that resolution by maintaining the structures of moral discourse in the community and by declaring herself to be an active party in that conversation. And this in itself is an exercise of leadership, as she begins the process of making sure the story of Christ is told in the center of the community.

Telling the story in the center is genuinely moral leadership because it demands that the story of the good be told and lived out in the working relationships of the community. It insists that there is a moral dimension to all the activities of the minister in pursuing her or his vocation of forming the character of the people of God. Telling the story in the center should not be disparaged as a less glamorous, less direct form of leadership compared to the varieties of transforming leadership to be discussed below. In fact, it often precedes them as it establishes the credibility and solidarity of the leader with those he or she seeks to move.

Yet there are serious temptations facing those who tell the story in the center—and that means facing every minister at some time or another. We can get so embroiled in the transactional brokering of interests as to lose our critical angle of vision on whether those interests truly represent the deeper story of the community. We can be tempted by bureaucracy and the maintenance of structures for their own sake.[10] We can get so enmeshed in the day-to-day demands of the community that we lose our ability to hear other voices calling. We can be tempted by success, enjoying the reputation of being a minister who "gets things done" and not taking on conflicts where success is not ensured or where more transforming leadership is called for.

Perhaps most of all, we are tempted by what seems a

reasonable caution. The associate minister at the social concerns meeting might find herself saying, "I can't take this on now. I must wait until I know more about this community's story, until I'm better established with the power bases here." This is especially dangerous because it has an element of truth in it. She must have at least one foot in the center of the community in order to move it. The problem is we would all like to wait until we have both feet firmly rooted, and by that time we may be so heavily invested in the status quo that the pull to the center makes it impossible to go out on the edge, even to tell the story in the center. This is the point at which she might rationalize: "Well, I'm really called to be a preacher and pastor for these folk. Someone else must be called to be a moral leader." In saying this, she would not only fail to see the moral dimensions of the everyday preaching and pastoring of the minister, she would also fail to see that "someone else" is not there and may never arrive.[11]

For the truth is that if we cannot bring ourselves to tell the story truthfully in the center, we will never be able to tell it from the edge. It may be that much of the day-to-day work of a minister is transactional in a very mundane sense, servicing the network of relationships that make up the life of the community. But such transactional leadership has definite moral dimensions, because how it takes place depends on the larger vision of community held by those who engage in it, and what it preserves is the opportunity for the story of the community to play a forceful part in its everyday life. Telling the story in the center is the necessary groundwork for sustaining the community and for building a base for more radically transforming leadership.

In other words, ministers sooner or later discover that the time for which we have been preparing ourselves to lead has already arrived. It cannot be put off for a time in which we are "better prepared." But here the difference between telling the story *in* the center and telling it *from* the center becomes crucial. If we thought we had to wait until we could tell the story *from* the center, we would not only have to wait a long time, but we would also find ourselves telling it from the perspective of the center. It would not be the story of Christ, as it comes to this particular community, but instead the story of that community as it sees Christ. As the pastor watching the well-capping has already observed, those can be two very different stories indeed. If we think of ourselves as telling the story *in* the center, we preserve a sense of difference between the story we bring as one called by God to minister and the story of the people in which that vocation is exercized. We should also, then, feel less pressure to wait until we are established in the center and greater freedom to let the truth be carried by the story of Christ. That is a story we must always be ready to tell, however halting and imperfect our telling might be.

Telling the Story on the Edge

Earlier we overheard Paul telling the story in the center, but I think most people would agree he spent the greater part of his time telling it on the edge. Ironically enough, we meet him on the edge of Jerusalem, holding the clothes of those about to stone Stephen (Acts 7:59). We encounter him again on the outskirts of Damascus, about to receive a call that would put him forever on the edge of the Jewish community from which he had come (Acts 9:3ff.). And we hear his voice principally in letters written from afar, from the edge of communities where, even when he had been present, he had been a wayfarer with the dust of one town on his clothes and the sight of another in his mind's eye.

Yet Paul was more than physically on the edge. The story he told kept him theologically on the edge of the Hellenistic communities he traveled among. He lived at the intersection of communities, whether Jewish or Gentile, pagan or Christian. It is little wonder that, living on the edge, caught in the conflict of stories, Paul would tell the story of Christ as one that transformed the ordinary with a new vision: "While the Jews demand miracles and the Greeks look for wisdom, we are preaching a crucified Christ: to the Jews an obstacle they cannot get over, to the gentiles foolishness, but to those who have been called, whether they are Jews or Greeks, a Christ who is both the power of God and the wisdom of God" (I Cor. 1:22-24). More than Jews and Greeks have found the story of Christ a foolish stumbling block, especially when they have heard it told on the edge of their communities. Although we don't know the time and place Paul wrote to the Corinthians, we know that on 16 April 1963 another minister of the gospel wrote an open letter from the Birmingham city jail, addressed to eight white Alabama clergymen who had written him an open letter in January of that year, declaring his strategy disturbing and his tactics inflammatory.

Martin Luther King, Jr., began his reply with "My dear Fellow Clergymen."[12] His closing remarks opened with "I hope this letter finds you strong in the faith." In between he explains why he has come to Birmingham from Atlanta, saying that as Paul went out from Tarsus, "I too am compelled to carry the gospel of freedom beyond my particular hometown. Like Paul, I must constantly respond to the Macedonian call for aid." He recalls the history of racial segregation in Birmingham and the perpetual frustrations of blacks advised to "wait" until gradual social change materializes. He cites Reinhold Niebuhr's dictum that society is more immoral than its individuals. He defends civil disobedience by appealing to Augustine, Aquinas, Martin Buber, Paul Tillich, the Constitution of the United States, the book of Daniel, Socrates, the resistance to Hitler, and Hungarian freedom fighters.

King expresses his deep disappointment with white moderates who claim to be sympathetic yet whose lukewarm support and cautionary pronouncements hurt worse than the open hatred of the segregationists. Accused of being an extremist, he says, "I gradually gained a bit of satisfaction" from the company the accusation put him in, for "was not Jesus an extremist in love," Amos in justice, Paul for the gospel, Martin Luther for faith, John Bunyan for conscience, Lincoln and Jefferson for democracy?

But he writes that his greatest disappointment is with the leadership of the white churches, for among them, as ministers of the gospel, he had hoped to find his strongest support, but instead found the country "moving toward the exit of the twentieth century with a religious community largely adjusted to the status quo." He reports traveling over the South, admiring "her beautiful churches with their lofty spires pointing heavenward," but he muses, "Over and over again I have found myself asking, 'What kind of people worship here? Who is their God?' . . . Yes, I see the church as the body of Christ. But, oh! How we have blemished and scarred that body through social neglect and fear of being nonconformists." King expresses the hope that the church may abandon its "silent and often vocal sanction of things as they are" but is sure the civil rights movement will go forward, with the church or without it. The demand for freedom is closely bound to the "sacred heritage of our nation and the eternal will of God."

Approaching his conclusion, King notes that the white preachers had "warmly commended" the Birmingham police for their conduct during the strike. He tries to turn their vision away from the police and toward the demonstrators their dogs attacked and their jailers mistreated, toward the blacks, young and old, who put their bodies on the line for human freedom and away from police administrators who acted with restraint only to preserve an immoral system. Then, after asking their understanding for the unseemly length of his letter ("What else is there to do when you are alone for days in the dull monotony of a narrow jail cell other than write long letters, think strange thoughts, and pray long prayers?"), he writes: "If I have said anything in this letter that is an overstatement of the truth and is indicative of an unreasonable impatience, I beg you to forgive me. If I have said anything in this letter that is an understatement of the truth and is indicative of my having a patience that makes me patient with anything less than brotherhood, I beg God to forgive me." [13]

These words and what has preceded them give a compelling clarity to his valedictory remark, "I hope this letter finds you strong in the faith." In calling his readers to a renewed accountability for what their faith demands of them and in giving them the courage by example and exhortation to live out those demands in trying times, King reminds us that telling the story on the edge exhibits many characteristics of what we might call a prophetic ministry. Earlier in discussing images of the minister, I did not list "prophet" as a separate image, though the words of prophets fill the Hebrew Scriptures and the leadership of prophets, women and men, appears throughout the literature of earliest Christianity.[14] I have not isolated the image of prophet because the exercise of prophetic ministry is so much a part of all the activities of the minister as moral leader as to be inseparable from it. Telling the story on the edge is the task of a prophetic preacher, a prophetic teacher, a prophetic priest, pastor, or servant. It is vitally important to think of the prophetic as a pervasive quality of moral leadership, lest we yield to the temptation to compartmentalize prophetic ministry as "someone else's job." It is precisely this culpable lack of vision on the part of the white church leadership that King so strongly lamented in his letter from jail.

Put this way, we can see the leader telling the story on the edge not as one who prophesies in the popular sense of *foretelling* the future but as one who exercises what Walter Brueggemann has called "prophetic imagination" and is engaged in the much more daunting task of *transforming* the future. The task prophetic imagination undertakes, according to Brueggemann, is "to nurture, nourish, and evoke a consciousness and perception alternative to the consciousness and perception of the dominant culture around us." A leader so engaged in telling the story on the edge, in other words, "is called to be a child of the tradition, one who has taken it seriously in the shaping of his or her own field of perception and system of language, who is so at home in that memory that the points of contact and incongruity with the situation of the church in culture can be discerned and articulated with proper urgency."[15]

Brueggemann goes on to say that the chief activities of this prophetic imagination are the critical dismantling of the dominant consciousness and the corresponding energizing of "persons and communities by its promise of another time and situation toward which the community of faith may move." This is accomplished by evocative lamentations for the present corruption of consciousness, and the amazed announcement of a vision of restoration and new creation. This capacity to feel both strong grief and powerful amazement in a culture prone to the quiet death of the status quo is at the heart of a truly prophetic ministry.[16]

All of these features are visible in King's remarkable letter. He exhibits prophetic imagination as the capacity to recall lost or suppressed parts of the story and to envision alternative realities to the way the story is told from the center. In doing so he shows himself to be thoroughly grounded in the images and figures of the story and capable of providing a fresh angle of vision on how that story should be told today. He moves to turn the vision of his people from one way of viewing the world to another. Although he criticizes the dominant consciousness in detail, he also offers an energizing vision of the possibilities inherent in living out the Christian story, with all its socially radical implications for the present age.[17]

King challenged the conventional telling of the story by white church leaders, but more than that, he challenged their identity in a way that also called into question the character of all who would call themselves Christian. "What kind of people worship here? Who is their God?" Telling the story from the edge always questions the character of the community.

The minister on the telephone heard a parishioner on the edge, lamenting her shattered world. Instead of being energized to assist her in moving forward into an alternative future, however, he reacted by trying to protect his own identity and his center-dominated perception of the character of his community: "For God's sake, don't tell anyone in the church." Who is the minister's God? What kind of people worship in that God's church? The voice from the edge, whether a leader's or a follower's, is a voice full of dangerous opportunities.

The minister watching the well-capping is confronted in a number of ways with telling the story on the edge. He is able to see the situation as being out of character with the deep story of his community, because at one time or another he himself heard the Christian story told on the edge. He heard it from a preacher in his youth, who told the story of the good Samaritan with a challenge to the congregation always to ask who the set-upon travelers in their lives are and whether they themselves respond as good Samaritans. He heard it from a teacher in seminary, who helped him read King's "Letter" not as an item of academic interest but as a sharply posed question addressed far more widely than to those eight Alabama pastors. He heard it from a small minority of his present congregation, who had been participating in an interfaith, interracial youth ministry, much to the displeasure of most of the church. He heard it watching the well-capping, as he recalled another Samaritan and another well and Jesus saying

Whoever drinks this water
will be thirsty again;
but no one who drinks the water that I shall give him
will ever be thirsty again:
the water that I shall give him
will become in him a spring of water, welling up for eternal life.

(John 4:13-14)

The minister stood in a line of storytellers handing on in their words and actions the story of Christ, the love of God and neighbor. The fearful realization that came to him at his study window was that the line had come down to him. It was his turn to tell the story on the edge, and his worst fear came from the realization that this was not simply an insight about a *decision* he had to make. It was instead an insight about what kind of *person* he was and what kind of leader he was called by God to become. Just as anything he would say or do would call into question the character of his community, so did this very realization call his own character into question. He had to ask himself, both literally and metaphorically, what well he would drink from now.

In other words, the minister will find that telling the story on the edge is inevitably a transforming experience. It transforms those who speak and those who hear, for they can never again stand in the same relation to each other unless they move together toward a transformed destination. And as King observed in his letter, it is impossible to wait until the "time" is right for such a move. It is, in fact, "the times" that are so often intransigent.

A long process of formation, dependent on telling the story in the center, lies behind the possibility of transformation. Telling the story in the center keeps alive the chance to tell it on the edge, where the consciousness of conflict that gives rise to transformation is most keenly felt. The more intense the conflict, however, the more transformation may be called for in order to overcome the intransigence of the times. The minister at the well-capping knows he cannot respond simply by telling the story in the center, for part of the problem is how the Christian story has been heard in that center in those times. He comes to see that he must tell the story on the edge, as he has heard it himself, but he knows he cannot simply repeat what he has heard. The voice of his preacher and teacher can speak in the present only through him, and the voices of that active minority in his congregation have already spoken and not been heard. The prophetic activity of lamenting and energizing may well not produce an alternative vision powerful enough for the times. A greater degree of transformation may be called for, one that tells the story even more radically on the edge, out where other voices, other stories are heard. It may be time not to talk *about* a good Samaritan but, as Jesus did at the well, to talk *with* one.

Hearing New Voices, Telling New Stories

It is perhaps ironic and certainly fearful that leadership at its most transforming breaks down boundaries and forms new communities in their wake. The leaders living most fully on the edge are those who can hear new voices and tell new stories. Such leaders hear the voices of those in their own community who have been thrust so far out on the edge as to be invisible to the center. They hear the voices of other communities witnessing to the story of the good that leads them on. Most profoundly (and most disturbingly), they hear voices that make telling new stories inevitable and cast such a new light on reality that transformation is irrevocable even where its implications are incompletely worked out. None of the great and compelling stories that give order to our complex world are told in one voice. One of the things that keeps great leaders on the edge is their capacity, sometimes experienced as a curse, to hear new voices and tell new stories.[18]

We have heard Paul telling the story in the center and on the edge. We see him wrestling with Jewish, Gentile, and Christian communities, exercising forceful leadership on matters of corporate solidarity and individual faith. He was launched on this journey when he heard a new voice, and responded by telling a new story. It was characterized by a radical simplicity, amazing in its richness and terrifying in its implications. "So for anyone who is in Christ, there is a new creation: the old order is gone and a new being is there to see" (II Cor. 5:17).

Years later, Coretta Scott King would say of her husband's most famous speech, "At that moment it seemed as if the Kingdom of God appeared. But it only lasted for a moment."[19] In that moment, Martin Luther King told a new story in response to the new voice he had heard, a voice that told of a possibility at the time so startling that in telling about it King could not declare a present reality but only report an amazing dream.

> So I say to you, my friends, that even though we must face the difficulties of today and tomorrow, I still have a dream. It is a dream deeply rooted in the American dream that one day this nation will rise up and live out the true meaning of its creed—we hold these truths to be self-evident, that all men are created equal.
>
> I have a dream that one day on the red hills of Georgia, sons of former slaves and sons of former slave-owners will be able to sit down together at the table of brotherhood. . . .
>
> I have a dream that one day every valley shall be exalted, every hill and mountain shall be made low, the rough places shall be made plain, and the crooked places shall be made straight and the glory of the Lord will be revealed and all flesh shall see it together. . . .
>
> And when we allow freedom to ring, when we let it ring from every village and hamlet, from every state and city, we will be able to speed up that day when all of God's children—black men and white men, Jews and Gentiles, Catholics and Protestants—will be able to join hands and to sing in the words of the old Negro spiritual, "Free at last, free at last; thank God Almighty, we are free at last."[20]

Paul did not fully work out the shape of the new creation. His letters contain a curious mix of eschatological vision and practical advice on daily Christian living. His treatment of slaves differed from his treatment of slavery. His seeming adherence to a patriarchal dominance of men over women cannot be squared with his declaration of their equality in Christian freedom and his own grateful reliance on female co-workers. Martin Luther King's inspiring vision of America as a land of genuine freedom and equality is expressed for the most part in language that some people then and many people today would call sexist, with its talk of brotherhood and the rights of men. Were he alive today, King might well have heard the new voices of women and told stories of the liberation of women from the oppression of men, just as in his lifetime he began to hear voices beyond the civil rights movement and to tell stories of the tragedies of Vietnam and nuclear war.[21]

It is not always easy to know what the new creation looks like or to see what is being pointed to when a prophetic voice says, "Look, I am doing something new, now it emerges; can you not see it?" (Isa. 43:19). The radical transformation brought on by hearing new voices and telling new stories is a part of life on the edge that will always remain frightful and empowering, unsought for and desired. The minister as moral leader must cultivate the capacity to be an agent of imagination, envisioning new directions of movement and new partners for the journey in moving the people of God toward the destination of their restless hearts. At times this will be so challenging to the way the story is told in the center that it sunders the community into those who accept and those who reject the new telling of the story. The alternative vision of what the community is called to become may be far from what the community has been, requiring a transformation so great that the challenge of leadership is not only to point to the new thing God is doing but also to teach the people of God to see in the first place. Nowhere is it more evident that such a task requires the transformation of leaders and followers alike.

Linda, whom we left back in seminary, is becoming more and more aware of this dimension of life on the edge. She had always known that her desire to pursue ordained ministry put her beyond the edge of the Baptist and Roman Catholic churches she had come from. What she discovered in seminary was how marginalized she and all women had been in the wider history of the Body of Christ. She came to see King's image of that Body scarred by segregation as applicable to the scars of gender oppression as well. And she began to realize the radical degree of transformation that would be necessary for the healing of those wounds in the Body of Christ. It would require a transformation that would call her to be a different kind of leader than she had first imagined and that would call the Christian community to be a different kind of people than they thought themselves to be.

She had heard new voices that would demand and enable the telling of new stories. These voices came from many corners. She heard them in biblical studies, where she learned that God was a motherly creator and not just a fatherly judge, and that in Christ there is no male or female. She heard them in historical studies, where she studied the rise and mainte-nance of patriarchy as a cultural institution and was comforted by Julian of Norwich that all, somehow, shall be well. She heard them in theological studies, where models of God and human relationships were divested of centuries of sexist images. She heard them in psychology, where women spoke in a different voice of a caring, sustaining love, and in pastoral care, where the story of Christ was directed against sexual and domestic violence. She heard them in theological ethics, where consciousness and conscience were linked and human rela-tionships explored. She heard them in pastoral theology, where women preached the Word, offered at Table, prayed fresh prayers, and sought to lead in church and world.[22]

The more she heard, the more she became aware of a transformation already taking place within herself. She felt solidarity with her fellow students but realized they were a small group in what was after all a small part of a very large community. She became angry and had to find ways to transform anger into energy for change. She became depressed and had to find ways to cast aside despair in the face of little evidence for hope. She became scared, all the more so when she saw that the fear of meeting resistance to her ministry was, after all, a reasonable fear. But somehow she became inspired, as the testimony of those voices, that cloud of witnesses, made her aware that telling new stories was not only possible but absolutely necessary, and that the structures of the world could indeed be transformed, though not without great cost. She even found some inspiration in Paul, who reminded her that she must no longer judge even success and failure by the standards of this world. It was not without a certain amount of ironic amusement that, as a woman in ministry, she could confidently affirm Paul's claim, "It is not being circumcised or uncircumcised that matters; but what matters is a new creation" (Gal. 6:15).

Though Linda does not know it, she has a sister in ministry who is also undergoing transformation as she seeks to transform others in the name of Christ. The student pastor, whose gay friend had asked for the use of a room in the church building for a ministry to persons with AIDS, certainly finds herself trying to lead on the edge. Aware of her own marginalization, she is sensitive to other voices on the edge and so hears the plea of her friend. She realizes that taking a stand on this is a risky business. As a student pastor, she has little standing in the first place, and though she wants to reject the patriarchal hierarchy that gives pride of place to those "above," she knows she would certainly "pay" for open opposition to her senior pastor. She feels morally unable to stand still and pragmatically unable to move. She has to overcome anger at her pastor and the church and self-reproach for trying to work "within the system" and thus putting herself in such a bind. She has more than enough of the consciousness of conflict necessary for the possibility of movement. What she needs is some new voice announcing a *way* to move out of her conflicted impasse.

Sometimes the new voices we hear are old voices heard for the first time in concert with others. The student pastor went home in great frustration. As was her practice at the end of the day, she sat down to read Scripture, though she was so distracted that it took her by surprise when she realized the reading for the day was the story of the Syro-Phoenician woman in Mark 7:24-30. As she read this familiar story, she found it speaking to her in a new voice, and with growing excitement heard that it had a great deal to say about the situation she was in or, more precisely, about the situation she, the pastor, and the church were in. The story spoke to her not just about AIDS but about the exhilaratingly difficult task of becoming the new creation.

What she began to reflect on was this. She had frequently heard persons with AIDS compared to New Testament lepers, repugnant and socially outcast victims of disease and fear. The suggestion, which might well have been made by her pastor, was that just as Jesus took pity on lepers, so Christians today should take pity on AIDS "victims." Although this analogy was usually well meant and often stirred reluctant people to respond at least privately, she had begun to realize from conversations with her gay friend that it was fundamentally misleading. For although our initial reactions to them are often the same, he argued that AIDS sufferers are significantly different from New Testament lepers. Persons with AIDS are not always disfigured, especially in the early stage of infection, nor are they outcast simply because of their disease. They often come from groups already socially marginalized, so that if they were healed miraculously overnight many people would still find them deviant. Her friend admitted that many people do tend to see AIDS "victims" as lepers, as polluting society, as "unclean" and therefore contaminating everything they touch. But he pointed out that this was probably not true of what passed for leprosy in New Testament times, and in any case it had been repeatedly established that it is not true of AIDS. He argued that education about transmission paths and common sense preventive measures are far more appropriate than hysteria about casual contact or proposals for massive quarantine. He suspected that what people really see as "unclean" is that AIDS chiefly afflicts people society already thinks of as "moral lepers" anyway, and that comparing them to real lepers is just another way to isolate the sufferers while assuaging the consciences of "good" members of society.[23]

Recalling that conversation while reading the Gospel of Mark, she began to think she had much more radical things to learn from Jesus about AIDS by observing how he responded to the Syro-Phoenician woman. For persons with AIDS suddenly seemed more like her than like the lepers of popular imagination. Like the Syro-Phoenician woman, persons with AIDS are already outcast before they might be sick. Like her, they often look "normal" except in our moral vision. It is even the case, she thought, that we often encounter their needs through the supplications of other people, as Jesus hears the Syro-Phoenician pleading on behalf of her daughter. But most important, the student began to realize that in reaching out to AIDS sufferers, one is transformed, as Jesus found in responding to the woman at the well.

The student pastor observed that Mark puts the story of the Syro-Phoenician woman at the start of Jesus' journeys outside the familiar confines of Galilee. He encounters her against his will, in the alien territory of Tyre. "There he went into a house and did not want anyone to know he was there; but he could not pass unrecognised. At once a woman whose little daughter had an unclean spirit heard about him and came and fell at his feet" (Mark 7:24-25). She begs him to heal her daughter, and he tells her in what must have been a sharp tone that the "children" (among whom she evidently did not number) should be fed first, rather than the "dogs" (among which she did). Here, the student pastor thought, was the segregation of the good and the deviant, the favored and the outcast, that works today in many Christians' response to those with AIDS.

Then an astounding thing happens: "But she spoke up. 'Ah yes, sir,' she replied, 'but little dogs under the table eat the scraps from the children'" (Mark 7:28). In a remarkable show of courage and determination, she turns Jesus' metaphor around on him, showing him that even within its own boundaries he has not given her what is rightfully due. And just as remarkably, Jesus, instead of defensively reinterpreting the image or rebuking her for talking back, replies instead: "For saying this you may go home happy; the devil has gone out of your daughter" (Mark 7:29). The student realized that the author of Mark may have had some polemical aims here, showing that the Samaritans recognized Jesus' power. But she found it nonetheless remarkable to see someone correcting Jesus and getting away with it, not only without rebuke but with his blessing.[24]

Sitting there at her kitchen table, she realized with a great burst of energizing amazement that if Jesus can learn from a Syro-Phoenician woman, who in her need challenged his conception of who he was in relation to the people to whom he was sent, surely she, her pastor, and the church can learn from those suffering from AIDS something about who we all are in relation to the God who has sent us and about the painful and uncertain world that holds our mission. She asked herself, What would Christians be known by today, that they could not pass unrecognized? Are we people who can face the truth about who is sick and who is well? About why others suffer and why we should suffer in solidarity with them? About the love and mercy God has shown to us, that we might in turn show it to others? She realized that our response to these questions is a test and a sign of whether our character as Christians truly embodies God's presence in the world. And she was empowered by remembering that trying to lead the people of God toward that embodiment was why she felt called to ministry in the first place.

As luck would have it, next Sunday was "Youth Ministry Day," and she would have her first opportunity in two months to preach. For the first time she felt glad that her congregation did not strictly follow the lectionary. She got up to fix herself some coffee and to find a pen and paper.

What Linda and her sister in ministry are discovering is that the Christian story is never told in one voice. Indeed, "the Christian story" is itself a collection of stories. It is no accident that the canon of the Christian Scriptures was formed over time from a variety of stories, that some were included and others left out, and that this took place with the strange mix of happenstance and intentionality that marks all historical processes.[25] Telling the Christian story proceeds in a similar way today. New voices with fresh metaphors and images speak for people whose lives and experiences have been lost or suppressed in the voice of the dominant narrative.

The capacity to hear and respond to new voices underlies the ability of the minister as moral leader to tell the story in the center of the community and to tell it in prophetic witness on the edge. But the temptation not to listen to new voices is great.

Leaders who hear new voices and tell new stories find themselves on the edge of their communities whether they want to be there or not, as the student pastor became increasingly aware in confronting the conflicting voices of her own center and edge. The temptations to shut out those voices, to withdraw from telling the story in the center or on the edge, are continual and often compelling. They represent the comforting but deadly pull to the center. Against Paul's declaration of a new creation, the center would assure us the world as we know it is not in need of any fundamental change. Against the insistence of Martin Luther King, the center would have us wait a little longer to see if the trouble would pass. Against the dangerous voices of women, which Linda has begun to hear, the center would tell us those are the complaints of a discontented few who need only to embrace the center fully to be fulfilled. And against that amazement of Jesus at the faith of the Syro-Phoenician woman, the center would tell us that new voices must be stilled, that only old voices tell the truth, that madness surely lies down the path of new voices and new stories.

In daring to take that path, we will do well to remember some words of Paul. He always insisted on his own authority to tell the new story of Christ and on the risks he had born in telling the story in the center and on the edge of many diverse communities. Yet Paul never forgot whose story it was, why he was telling it, and whose Spirit moved through the story to open the hearts of those who heard it.

> For what is Apollos and what is Paul? The servants through whom you came to believe, and each has only what the Lord has given him. I did the planting, Apollos did the watering, but God gave growth. In this, neither the planter nor the waterer counts for anything; only God, who gives growth. It is all one who does the planting and who does the watering, and each will have the proper pay for the work that he has done. After all, we do share in God's work; you are God's farm, God's building.
>
> By the grace of God which was given to me, I laid the foundations like a trained master-builder, and someone else is building on them. Now each one must be careful how he does the building. For nobody can lay down any other foundation than

the one which is there already, namely Jesus Christ. (I Cor.
3:5-11)

Paul was a person of great intellect and vision but of a
surprisingly mundane imagination. His stock of metaphors
exhausts itself with the body, the sports field, and the daily
round of agriculture. Here he cannot even stick to one
metaphor. Watering the garden, he sees the farm buildings
and lets us know we are both crop and silo. Beyond what I have
quoted here, the farm buildings will remind him of temples,
and this of his favorite metaphor, the body: "You are that
temple" (I Cor. 3:17). But the point of all of this is clear,
perhaps clearer for the mix of metaphors, each rushing to
express something too complex and important to be contained
in one alone, so that I may be excused for shifting metaphors
once again.

We tell the story, but God tells us. We are God's words to one
another, and our very telling becomes a new voice and a new
story to be told again by others long after we are silent at the
last. Paul is reminding us that the minister as moral leader is by
no means the minister as *savior*. That role in the story is already
filled. We have in the present age more obligation to try and
less to succeed because of the efforts of those planters and
builders before us and the vocations of those to come, for the
same God calls all the workers. If we trust in this, we can be
bold in the telling and confident in the hearing the story will
receive.

CHAPTER 5

THE TEMPTATION NOT TO LEAD

The apostle Paul was no stranger to conflict. He frequently faced opposition, and as Luke reports it, expected those who became leaders after him to face it as well. "I know quite well that when I have gone fierce wolves will invade you and will have no mercy on the flock. Even from your own ranks there will be [people] coming forward with a travesty of the truth on their lips to induce the disciples to follow them" (Acts 20:29-30).

But Paul, like the leaders who follow him, faced other challenges to leadership. There are quieter but not less crippling threats that come from the tangled relationship of leaders to particular historical communities and from the paralyzing fears and misgivings that often afflict the minister. Such entanglements and fears tempt us not to lead and prevent us, whether out of myopic blindness or personal fright, from taking up the risky path of transforming leadership. We can get a better idea of this temptation and an inkling of how it might be overcome by taking a closer look at Paul's complicated relationship with the Christians of Corinth.[1]

The Corinthian congregation was founded by Paul and his co-workers about 50 or 51 C.E. and seems to have specialized in conflict and misunderstanding as much as in works of love. Paul wrote his first (now lost) letter to the church sometime before 54 C.E. and in reply received a letter from the Corinthians and some independent oral reports to which he replies in I Corinthians toward the end of 54 C.E. Something seems to have gone badly wrong in the congregation that winter, for Timothy's report of his visit in the spring of 55 c.e. prompted an emergency trip by Paul, during which he seems to have had a traumatic encounter with a member of the congregation.

The plot thickens. Paul had evidently told the Corinthians he was going to pay them a "double visit" on his way to and from Macedonia (II Cor. 1:15-16). Instead of going in person, he sends what must have been a sharply worded letter (now lost) addressing the threat to his leadership as a threat to the integrity of the whole community and commanding the Corinthians to resolve the problem. This letter proved risky. It apparently succeeded in getting the Corinthians to punish the offender but also upset many of them with its harsh tone, and even more because Paul had done in writing what he had promised to do in person. Their reaction prompts Paul to write II Corinthians 1–9, expressing his pain and his fear of causing further pain, yet forcefully defending his actions. He urged reconciliation within the community and between it and himself and (as we saw in the last chapter) appealed to the Corinthians to show their solidarity and love by contributing to the collection Paul was organizing for the poor in Jerusalem. This letter may have resolved the original dispute, but it failed to quell criticism of Paul's personal authority. When Paul became aware of that, he dispatched the much sterner and more openly confrontational letter we have today as II Corinthians 10–13. We can only guess that Paul's leadership eventually won the day from Romans 15:26-27, which suggests that the Corinthians had finally contributed to the collection for Jerusalem, and from the fact that much of the letter to the Romans seems to have been written by Paul from Corinth.[2]

Paul had badly misread the historical setting of his ministry in Corinth and misjudged his own relationship to the community. Beset with fear and misgivings, he had been forced to lead from a defensive posture. His leadership had been shaped more by the accidents of history in which it occurred than by the destination he pursued. He had gotten out of touch with the people he was trying to lead and in doing so had in some crucial sense withheld his leadership, after which he had to scramble to reestablish it. I am going to leave Paul tangled up for now and take another look at his situation at the end of this chapter. In the meantime, let us look more closely at the temptation not to lead that arises when leaders are entangled and afraid.

Leadership Entangled

Leaders can become entangled in the accidents of history that have defined the communities they enter. They can become entangled in a variety of expectations of what image of the minister they should embody. Perhaps most difficult of all, they can become entangled in conflicting stories of the good that compete for the hearts of the communities they would lead. We can find each of these entanglements in the stories of leadership we have been following thus far.

The pastor watching the well-capping is thoroughly entangled in the accidents of history.[3] Such accidents of history are particular to *this* time and place. They are "accidental" because in a different time and place they might not even exist, yet here they constitute the arena of moral leadership. The well he is watching has been there a long time and has had practical and symbolic value in the community. The church responsible for capping it has had a long history of relations with the church our pastor represents and with the black community on the edge of town whose members had recently been using the well. Our pastor, new in the area, does not yet know the story of these relationships. For that matter, he is fairly ignorant of the story of what has now become "his" church. He is unsure, had the well been on his church's property, whether his parishioners would have capped it or not.

The complexities of the past do not end his entanglement in the accidents of history. He will also discover that his leadership is shaped by what is currently going on in the community. Does his church, or the one whose workers he watches, represent the center or the edge of the wider community? Are there movements afoot pulling either church toward the edge or the center? Are there well-defined power bases within the lay leadership whose interests provide a direction for the churches as a whole? All these things, past and present, entangle our pastor in the accidents of history before he can even understand how his church sees what is taking place, let alone how he could exercise effective moral leadership in the face of the offense to the gospel that *he* sees when he looks at the well-capping. In fact, the first task of the new leader is to find out what exactly is going on. Hearing the local story of *this* community is a necessary preface to telling the larger Christian story in the center or on the edge.[1]

No leader can escape this sort of entanglement, or the many hours of storytelling and hearing that will be required to come to some deeper awareness of these accidents of history. The real danger of this entanglement is not that it takes a lot of effort but that there is no easy way to know when listening and questioning must be set aside and more active leadership taken up. There will be many voices, for example, not the least of which will be the minister's own, urging our pastor "Don't get too involved until you know what's really going on." That is at the same time a genuine warning to become aware of the accidents of history and a possible rationalization for never challenging the status quo. This sort of entanglement ends in paralysis, because it destroys the confidence of the leader to let the story of the good life speak vividly to particular situations. Without a way through this entanglement, our pastor will watch the well-capping with a bitterness born of his conviction that he is not yet able to move forcefully and the fear he never will be.

Our ability to find a way through that paralysis is qualified by another sort of entanglement that has its roots in the often conflicting expectations placed on the role of the minister. These expectations come from the culture of the local community and the history of how ministers have lead there in the past. They come from the role of minister assumed by the corporate or institutional church that ordains or commissions the minister and from the intimate vision of ministry that forms the basis of an individual minister's vocation. These expectations may place severe restrictions on what images of *the minister*—preacher, teacher, pastor, priest, servant—any *particular* minister should take up, and how they should be lived out.

We can see this in the story of the student pastor. She is entangled in the conflicting expectations of her friend, her senior pastor, her church community, her denomination, her seminary, and her vocation. Her friend wants her to be a pastor to him and a servant to those with AIDS. Her senior pastor wants her to serve the church community in her public ministry and to pastor her friend privately. She feels ambiguous expectations from the church community. Does the pastor speak for the church? Does her friend? What would the church expect of her if it knew the details of her dilemma? She feels unspoken pressures from the institutional church that places her in a subordinate position to her senior pastor and that sends mixed signals on its vision of a Christian response to AIDS. Some of her seminary professors and fellow students urge her to be a prophetic preacher, teacher, and priest, standing up for the truth of the gospel as she sees it and opposing the status quo. The idea of providing leadership from the edge has great appeal, but it is clouded by her realization of how dependent she is on the powerful center represented by the institutional church. Her inner calling to love God and neighbor impels her to move toward leadership on the edge, at the same time that the corporate shaping of her vocation seems to restrict her range of movement to what can be accomplished within the present boundaries of the church that has made her a student pastor.

Her entanglement in expectations leads to a paralysis of leadership. It undermines her ability to see clearly the vision of the good that would guide the direction of her movement, because it challenges her confidence in answering the question of the servant, "Where does my allegiance lie?" Her desire to live a life of integrity, true to her calling, is made vastly more difficult by these conflicting expectations. She is tempted not to lead, because anything she might do would fail to live up to some of the expectations bearing down on her.

But alongside this entanglement lies still another. As the

minister responding to the anguished phone call and the associate presiding at the social concerns committee both discovered, we can become very entangled indeed in conflicting stories of the good and their different visions of what kind of people we are called to become. The woman calling her minister needed him to bring to her the Christian story of service to the oppressed and priestly reconciliation to the estranged. Instead, the minister responded out of a story that promised success to those who conformed to the center and did not threaten the status quo. In doing so he showed the suffering woman his true character, because he showed her which story of the good gave him direction when he was called on to lead. Perhaps he regretted what he said: perhaps it came from his own fear of conflict rather than from deep-seated allegiance to a story of defending the center. Sometimes our awareness of what story we *have* given our hearts to comes only when we act in character with the direction that story leads us and then reflect on whether that *is* in fact where we want to go.[5] We do not know whether that minister lay awake at night pondering his answer, or whether he thought the fact that she left the church was a good outcome to the incident. We do know the exchange raised the consciousness of conflicting stories of the good in the mind and heart of the woman, and that it set her in search of another community whose story could hear her tragedy and not turn away.[6]

The associate at the social concerns meeting was caught in the conflict of stories, but with a different twist. She was faced with two groups that each claimed authority for their positions from their hearing of the Christian story—a claim that tempted them to see the opposition not only as wrong but also as bad Christians. One group, whose members formed the center of that particular community, thought that to be Christian one had to oppose abortion *and* support capital punishment, and they could tell any number of biblical stories about eyes for eyes and teeth for teeth. The other group, represented by a lonely voice or two on the edge, thought that a consistently Christian pro-life position made it necessary to oppose abortion *and* capital punishment. This group could tell stories about loving the enemy and going the extra mile. All this made the associate minister's task of reconciliation much more difficult. She could not simply call both groups back to "the Christian story," for in large measure what was at stake was exactly the question of *what* the Christian story was, and what kind of people it should form.

She has discovered that the Christian story is never told in one voice and that the center and the edge of a Christian community will most likely tell it in voices difficult to harmonize. She may discover that transforming leadership must try to make different voices audible to one another, so that the ensuing conversation might enable the whole community to hear the story of the good in all its complex overtones. In this she will discover that the transformation necessary in the face of conflict and change requires her own transformation first of all, so that she can hear all the voices in the community along with the voice she heard calling her in her vocation to be a minister of a church that seeks to love God and neighbor. Hearing these many voices, she will try to help each hear the others, but as a transforming leader, she will have to risk declaring in what direction she hears this complex storytelling urging the community to move. Despite all her efforts at communication and reconciliation, such a declaration will inevitably put her at odds with some members of the church. All this she knows, as she becomes aware of the conflicting stories dominating that committee meeting. It should be no wonder that such entanglement might draw her, and us, into a paralyzing fear that makes leadership difficult or impossible.[7]

The three entanglements we have looked at are often themselves tangled together. As we learn about the accidents of history in a particular congregation, we may find we have inherited rigid role expectations that focus on one or two images of the minister. We may then discover that those images come from voices telling the Christian story at the center of the community and may conflict with voices telling it at the edge or with the calling that led us into ministry in the first place. We may also discover ourselves in conflict with other stories that would so drown out *any* telling of the Christian story as to keep it from threatening the status quo.

All these entanglements seem to have been at work in the lives of the Christian leaders to whom Martin Luther King, Jr., addressed his "Letter from Birmingham City Jail," as we saw in the last chapter. Their entanglement had paralyzed them out of fear of conflict and change and led them to withhold the leadership that King argued the Christian story so clearly called them to exercise. His telling of the story on the edge sought to transform them in the center, to help them break through paralysis to move as God calls Christians to move. In doing so we saw him asking them to consider what story actually formed their character, to reflect on whether they embodied the love of God and neighbor or the defense of property and the status quo. In order to understand the transformation of character involved in moving through our entanglements, we need to look more closely at how we can be tempted to withhold moral leadership, and at the underlying dispositions and fears that seem to give us reasons to hold back.

Leadership Withheld

In the examples above I have been speaking as if withholding leadership is something done by an individual leader. This is largely true. Leadership is always exercised or withheld by some particular people. A person takes action or refuses to do something. She listens attentively or turns a deaf ear to voices on the edge. He follows through on or withdraws from commitments already made. Yet looking at the larger context of the vocation of ministry, we can also say that institutions and communities exercise or withhold leadership. Such corporate bodies may take transforming public stands on issues like apartheid or nuclear disarmament, or they may refuse to go beyond the safer transactional boundaries of their own communities. They may actively seek to develop new leaders among their lay and ordained membership, or they may fail to keep even the everyday structures of moral discourse alive and functioning. They may respond to alternative tellings of their story with sensitivity and humility, or they may stubbornly refuse to take a critical look at their movement toward the good life.

A national church body or a local community can withhold leadership by failing to appoint leaders to existing ministries or failing to develop leadership in response to critical concerns, such as ministry to people with AIDS. Such institutions or communities can pressure ministers not to engage in transforming leadership on risky issues or to oppose leaders if they arise outside official lines of authority. Churches can fail to lead when they allow their own policies to be shaped by the demands of the social system upon which they rely for their continued existence. Where ministry is defined chiefly by the weight of tradition, the pressures of social conformity, and the capacity of a denominational retirement system, it becomes easier to find reasons to hold on to the center against the disruptive impulses of the edge.[8]

We can see some of the ways that groups and the individuals of which they are composed are tempted to withhold leadership, by looking at how the Roman Catholic community in which Linda discovered her vocation went about choosing a new minister. Linda's community was originally organized as a campus ministry at a large university. Though it focused on graduate and undergraduate students, the ministry had grown to become an active though unofficial parish community, including the families of faculty and staff and people from the surrounding neighborhoods who had been attracted to the lively diversity of the university setting.

When the nun who had been associate minister decided to leave campus ministry, a search for a new minister began. The incumbent priest, while officially the senior minister, wished to see the new associate minister hired under a job description that more closely reflected the collaborative leadership style that had emerged among himself, the woman leaving the post, and the lay leaders of the community. In consultation with the two ministers, the community council (an elected representative body) developed an appropriate job description.

Around this point in the process, an interesting thing happened. Although they had developed the description together and would be in charge of selecting, interviewing, and deciding among the prospective candidates, the members of the community council left it up to the clerical leadership to place the advertisement for the position in appropriate venues. The priest sent the advertisement to a professional campus ministry newsletter, and the nun placed it in a publication aimed at members of the religious order to which she belonged.

At a meeting six weeks later, when a list of candidates to be interviewed was supposed to be drawn up, the council was disturbed to discover that only two people had applied. When it came out that the ads had only been placed in two specialized publications, the council members were quite upset. Several people suggested that ads for an unusual position such as this should have gone into the wide-circulation religious press, where they would reach people interested in moving outside the traditional boundaries of campus ministry. After a long and somewhat difficult meeting, action was delayed on selecting candidates for interviews, and new ads were placed in broad-based, national publications. In the month after these ads appeared, eighteen new candidates responded. Eventually the new minister was chosen by the unanimous consent of a community council satisfied that it had had the chance to select the best of a strong and diverse group of candidates.

Where had leadership been withheld, and who held back? In many ways this was a successful process in the life of the community. A member of the community council at the time told Linda how proud she felt of being part of a decision that in another community might have been made by the church hierarchy alone. Yet she also told Linda that the process had uncovered a sort of passive clericalism, not so much on the part of the priest and the nun as deeply rooted among the lay council members. Letting the priest and the nun place the ads seemed the easiest thing to do. In fact, it was the *customary* thing to do, to let the official clerical leaders take charge and to withhold lay leadership on what turned out to be a crucial decision about where the community would actually find candidates willing to take on the unusual demands of the position.

After some reflection the council members did not think the

priest and nun had conspired to take leadership from the council. Nor did they blame specific council members for failing to exercise leadership. Instead, the council realized they had all failed to lead because they had all shared the mistaken assumption that "someone" would do the "right" thing. It was the council members as a group—which means it was each of them as individuals—who withheld leadership at a critical point. The clerical and lay members of the community had all fallen back on the same patterns of hierarchy that they had renounced in producing the job description. The experience of Linda's community is a sobering reminder of how groups as well as individuals can withhold leadership. It should also remind us that genuinely transforming leadership is difficult, not only because of the issues it tackles but also because of the demands for change it places on leaders and followers alike.

We can see from this story that although it is important to understand how leadership can be withheld, it is just as important to come to grips with the dispositions and fears that seem to give groups and individuals *reasons* for holding back. The temptation not to lead becomes especially powerful through the corrosive dispositions of complacency and wounded pride and through the paralyzing fear of change, failure, success, conflict, disapproval, and isolation.

A life formed too strongly by the forces of the center can shape ministers with a disposition to complacency. Complacency tempts us to withhold leadership because it leads us to close our eyes to problems we would rather not look at. It tells us everything is going smoothly and prevents us from checking in with dissenting voices on the edge of the complacent community. When we allow ourselves to become complacent, we enter a deadening self-deception that requires us to conspire with the status quo, lest we disrupt the arrangements that support our complacency. We tell ourselves it is "someone else's" job to integrate all the complex images of a minister in a vocation of moral leadership. Our job, we say, is to concentrate faithfully on the images most needed in our immediate congregation—which is to say, least disruptive to the status quo.

L. T. Matthiesen addresses the temptation to withhold

leadership out of complacency in a sermon on nuclear disarmament called "I Didn't Know the Gun Was Loaded."[9] The Roman Catholic bishop of Amarillo, Texas, Matthiesen lived fifteen miles away from Pantex, a factory that served as a final assembly point for thermonuclear warheads, and, in the early 1980s, for the neutron bomb. He had known the plant was there, but the knowledge had remained opaque until a member of his parish who worked at the plant came to him, troubled in conscience about producing the warheads. At about the same time there were other workers engaging in civil disobedience outside the plant and highly publicized local hearings on basing the MX missile system outside Amarillo. These events disrupted Bishop Matthiesen's complacency, "all introducing themselves on my heretofore largely untroubled world."

The bishop tells how he grew up in small Texas towns where guns were so common that scarcely anyone thought of their destructive potential. As he grew older, he began to hear stories of killings and accidental deaths. Once, hitting a pothole in a pickup truck while holding a rifle, he felt the gun fire and saw the bullet smash a window two inches from the driver's head. He felt lame and powerless as he said to his equally terrified friend, "I didn't know the gun was loaded." Such incidents led him to renounce the use of guns, but he later realized this had been a purely personal decision. It had not led him to question on a larger scale whether the guns of our society were loaded, and what they were loaded with.

> For thirty-three years I lived and continue to live at the very portals of Pantex, and for those thirty-three years I said nothing either as a priest or as Bishop—until a Catholic employee and his wife came to me with troubled consciences. . . . I had come to realize, with Martin Luther King, Jr., that the choice really is between non-violence and nonexistence. Finally, I could no longer say, "I didn't know the gun was loaded."

Bishop Matthiesen issued a public statement denouncing the assembly of the neutron bomb at Pantex and became active in the nuclear disarmament movement. Once his complacency had been shattered, his self-deception unmasked, he found he could no longer withhold leadership; more important, he no longer was tempted to do so. Life is at once more difficult and more vibrant on the other side of complacency; difficult because our ordinary moral arrangements are shattered, yet vibrant because we are transformed by the renewal of our minds and hearts and given new energy to disrupt the complacency of others.

> My task is to tell the story from the perspective of a man who believes in God, out of the conviction of a citizen whose nation boasts "In God We Trust," a searcher of the Scriptures that say, "Put up your sword, for those who live by the sword will die by the sword. Love your enemies. Do good to those who hate you.". . . We have no alternative but to raise our voices. . . . If we do not do so, then let us pray that somewhere somehow a survivor will be left to speak in our name, to say of us, "They didn't know the gun was loaded."

We can also be tempted not to lead when we are disposed toward a certain kind of wounded pride. Pride can be both a virtue and a vice, and in either guise it is powerfully complex. Pride may go before a fall, but we also know from the experience of blacks, women, and other oppressed peoples that without enough pride in who we are and who we are capable of becoming, we will not stride forcefully enough to risk a fall. Excessive pride, rather than tempting us not to lead, may well tempt us to power-wielding, because such pride breeds a haughtiness that neglects other people's needs and goals. As a virtue pride asks us to find strength in our story and confidence in ourselves as people called by that story, people, as Martin Luther King reminds us, whose God is able. As a vice pride turns us away from our story toward ourselves, teaching us to trust that we alone are able to handle anything. This is the excessive pride that cuts us of from the needs of other people. But there lies in it a wounded pride that not only blinds us from the reality of other people but also prevents us from seeing our own limits and tempts us to a prideful insistence that we are capable of doing more than we actually can. In that situation, our reluctance to share power and leadership in the light of our own insufficiencies actually becomes a way of withholding leadership, for we neither provide leadership ourselves nor allow it to arise from others. When we run up against our limits, our wounded pride leads us to hold the needs of our communities hostage to what we alone can handle, whether or not events demand more than we can give.[10]

The temptation to withhold leadership out of wounded pride might have been operating in some of the scenarios we explored for the congregation trying to decide what to do with its unexpected legacy. The doors opened by the gift led to new possibilities for the church, but they also revealed distinct and sometimes conflicting groups whose goals were not easily reconciled. The senior pastor found it necessary to enlist the help of many lay leaders to ensure that the congregation as a whole had a real opportunity to participate in the decision about the legacy. What if he had reacted to the news of the gift by pridefully assuming this was a situation he could or should handle by himself? As matters got more and more complex, he would have been tempted to withhold active leadership that brokered the interests of the whole community because of the intimidating efforts such leadership would require. He would have become vulnerable to manipulation by a smaller group of power-brokers in the congregation who could have maneuvered the situation to their own benefit while preserving (for him as well as for the church) the illusion of the pastor's leadership. In fact, such wounded pride might well have fueled the scenario in which the pastor kept the news to himself and a small circle of powerful members, who then "packaged" the proposals to the congregation. Wounded pride led the pastor not to lead.

In addition to the dispositions of complacency and wounded pride, ministers can be tempted not to lead by a number of paralyzing fears. For leaders called to be transforming, one of the worst of these fears is the fear of change itself. As we saw in looking at the struggle between the center and the edge, it is part of our common human condition that we fear change. Transforming leaders are exactly those people who can overcome this fear in themselves and enable others to face the future confident that they enter times of change with the hope of a people whose ultimate destination remains true. Without that risky confidence, complacency tells us everything is fine just the way it is, and the fear of change only reinforces the message.

Here two other fears arise to make transformation even more difficult to risk. When we are complacent about the present and fear the prospect of change, we begin to fear for the failure *or* the success of our leadership in situations that call for transformation. Either failure or success will bring a change, a realignment of the status quo, will leave some members of the community pleased and others displeased or dispossessed. As we find ourselves stretched beyond our limits in new situations, we become fearful of being able to repeat the successful leadership we may have exercised in the past. We are tempted to withhold leadership, staying away from situations or controversies where we see more chances of failure than of success. Yet we are also tempted not to lead because success, along with the change it brings, makes the specter of future failure all the harder to bear. The more we succeed, the more our followers expect us never to fail, and the more we are tempted to lower our sights on how we exercise leadership to protect ourselves from failure. Finally, and more fearful still, success or failure forces us to examine the standards by which we measure either one. We may well fear to discover that our standards have more to do with the story of the world than the story of Christ.[11]

Fear of change, failure, and success afflicts the senior pastor of the church with the legacy. He had been resting complacently in the center of his community before the legacy opened up a rush of possibilities whose disruptive consequences he feared to face. He feared he would not be able to resolve the situation, and, his efforts ending in failure, his effectiveness as a leader would be seriously impaired, not to speak of his personal reputation. In fact, he was also afraid of success, for he realized that if he was to judge a particular outcome as a failure or success, he would have to engage in far more critical reflection on where his leadership was leading the church than his smooth course of the past few years had required. He was tempted to abandon leadership to power-wielders in the church rather than have to come to grips with what failure *or* success meant.

Such fears also afflicted the minister who counseled the woman with marital difficulties to keep quiet and tell no one in the church. He feared the disruptive changes that would inevitably come from the public acknowledgment of serious problems between two pillars of the church. He probably feared his own capacity to handle the disruption. He might have known other ministers whose leadership foundered on similar crises. He may have been avoiding deep scriptural and theological reflection on divorce, telling himself such things didn't happen to "good Christians." Yet such reflection would have been necessary before he could properly evaluate any outcome of his ministry. Would it be a success or a failure if this woman left her marriage or stayed in it? Whatever the outcome, if she felt helped by him, would that open the floodgates for other wounded spouses to come to him? Could be handle that? Could the church take such disruption? In any case, he recoiled from engaging in ministry with this woman, defending what he felt to be safe against what he feared to be dangerous.

We can also see at work in these examples the temptation to withhold leadership out of fear of conflict. The temptation to back away from conflict is not unusual. Like the fear of change, it is not without a good deal of survival value. Not all conflicts need to be faced directly, and knowing when to press and when to demur is an important part of the virtue of prudence that the minister as moral leader needs to develop.[12] Nonetheless, as we saw earlier, the possibility of movement arises out of the consciousness of conflict. No one aspiring to be a transforming leader—and that is an aspiration the vocation of ministry requires—can avoid the possibility of disruptive and unsettling conflict. In fact, whatever else they are, successful leaders are those who transform the sharpest conflicts into constructive movement toward the destination of the heart.[13]

The fear of conflict is made all the more difficult when it is coupled with the fear of disapproval. As we saw in looking at the conflicting expectations in which ministers become entangled, we can be tempted to withhold leadership in situations where we feel that *anything* we do will displease *somebody*. We can be especially tempted when the others involved have a controlling interest in our paychecks or our self-esteem. The minister watching the well-capping knows that speaking out against it will put him in conflict with most of the members of his pastor-parish relations committee. Yet those are the very people he needs to keep happy for his stay at the church to be a successful part of his journey up the clerical career ladder. The associate minister at the social concerns committee meeting knows that she is being closely watched by people on both sides of the issues splitting the church. She very much wants to be liked and accepted, not simply because of her career but as an affirmation of her vocation that will contribute to her self-esteem. Both these ministers fear the social consequences and the personal rejection that would come along with disapproval, and that fear provides a powerful incentive not to lead.[14]

The senior pastor of the woman trying to respond to her friend with AIDS also is tempted to withhold leadership. He fears conflict with powerful members of the congregation, whom he does not wish to displease. Furthermore, his own self-esteem is identified with the social class and values of those parishioners. He would have a very hard time bringing himself to take a position threatening that identification and so tells his student pastor she can do anything she wants to help her friend as long as it does not publicly involve the church (or its pastor!) in controversial issues. His self-esteem is tied up with the expectations of his job and the demands of his career. Somewhere along the line from his student days to the present he accepted the notion that, if he was going to be liked, he had to be nice, avoid conflict, and follow the expectations of his congregation. This makes it easier to hold back than to take action when conflict is sure to result.

The student pastor in this situation is also tempted to withhold leadership from fear of conflict but is spurred toward action by her own sense of self-esteem. She depends on the approbation and good will of other people whom she is loathe to offend and knows any action she takes will put her in conflict with some of those people. She fears conflict with church members, the senior pastor, and her church superiors. Yet she also fears the loss of self-esteem that would come from turning her back on her friend. Such a refusal would reveal her to be less fully committed to her vocation than she thought she was, and that helps her push against the fear of conflict, for her self-esteem is grounded in faithfully living out the calling she has heard to love God and neighbor.

Perhaps her senior pastor started out that way as well. In her fear of conflict, the student pastor will no doubt be pressured to shift the grounds of her self-esteem away from her vocation toward the expectations of those in a position to judge her—and reward her. Perhaps she will even be tempted, as her senior pastor seems to have been, to redefine her vocation so that she can live it out and still be liked by those she serves. At the very least she will discover a great and disturbingly attractive temptation to withhold leadership on controversial matters in order to preserve the approval of those who would shape her vocation by controlling her career.

In these last stories we can see the temptation not to lead arising from a fear of isolation. This is not just the desire to be liked but the fear of being cut off from ordinary human relations in the trauma created by transforming leadership. It is hard to be out on the edge alone. We may be able to overcome complacency, pride, fear of change, failure, success, conflict, and disapproval, only to lose the heart to lead in confronting the threat of isolation. The more radical the transformation, the farther out on the edge we begin, to the point where many others, even our friends, may not be able to share the vision that is calling us forth. The prophetic aspect of all moral leadership cannot escape the personal reality of the trials in the desert all prophets seem to undergo. We recall that one of Martin Luther King, Jr.'s bleakest moments came alone at midnight at a kitchen table, where friends and supporters seemed very far away indeed in light of the death threats he had received. The situation was a challenge not just to his leadership skills but to his own sense of who he was and of what kind of person he was called to become. King found that the clarity possible in isolation comes only at a great and terrible personal cost, and only God's presence enabled him to endure.

In a less dramatic but no less telling way, the minister watching the well-capping faces a crippling isolation as the final temptation not to lead. He can imagine the active opposition of those implacably resolved not to change the status quo. But just as threatening, he can imagine being frozen out of the life of the community. He can picture himself going about his daily rounds with no more than grudging recognition from the people whose lives he, an outsider, disrupted. He can see, in the fevered imagination reserved for our innermost fears, the prospect of spending three or four years in a small town without a friend. What if he spends years there, committing himself to a position from which he cannot honorably back down but which he cannot continue to defend alone? What will sustain him in his isolation?

In the last few pages we have been looking at ministers tempted not to lead. The unavoidable entanglements of ministry, the dispositions of complacency and pride, and the wide range of fears that afflict the heart can bring leaders to a point of paralysis, where the movement so characteristic of transforming moral leadership seems impossible to initiate or sustain. Restless hearts scurry round and round the same point in time and space, desiring a destination but fearing the journey there. They long to move but are tempted to hold back; in holding back, they gradually lose the power to move. What can give Christian leaders the power to move, to resist the temptation not to lead?

The Power to Move

The power to move through entanglement and to resist the paralyzing temptation not to lead begins to come when we admit we are in fact powerless to do it on our own. It begins to come when we admit our need for the support of other restless hearts, and our deep longing for the love of God in which all hearts find rest. It begins to come when we recall that our authority for purposeful movement comes from the story through which God has called us rather than from the institutions and communities in which we respond. The testimony of Jesus in the garden of Gethsemane, Paul in the back streets of Corinth, and King in his midnight kitchen is that we are most empowered to break through entanglements and paralysis of all sorts when we affirm that it is not we alone who will succeed *or* fail and that we can never be cut off from the presence of God.

For it is when we forget the story that called us into ministry in the first place that we place a misguided importance on our own success or failure, or on the expectations placed on us by people in a particular time and place. The story of Christ began in a certain time and place long ago, but it has been told and continues to be told in many places over many times. The minister as moral leader is entrusted with the retelling of the story in the present age, but exactly because it is a story of and for the ages, it is not one that can become the property of any one person or group trying to live it out. In the next chapter we will look at the terrible results of such a narrowing or twisting of the story God tells in us through Christ. For now we should realize that our ability to resist the temptation not to lead lies in the freedom from ultimate success or failure granted to us in the vocation we have received from God, and in our constant dependence on the support of others whose hearts yearn for God.

For just as there can be a corporate withholding of leadership, so can there be a corporate exercise of it. This may include specifically collaborative leadership, such as copastoring or team ministries. But I am urging us to go beyond those understandings of corporate leadership to the point where even an individual far out on the edge can think of himself or herself as surrounded by a cloud of witnesses. I am asking, for example, that we think of what happened in Linda's community as an occasion where the corporate exercise of leadership eventually overcame the corporate withholding of it. I am asking that we think of Jesus at Gethsemane, Paul in Corinth, and King in his kitchen as being supported by the presence of God but also by sleepy disciples, co-workers in the gospel, and transformed nonconformists.

Such an understanding of corporate leadership requires a strong sense of self, grounded in response to an individual vocation, and a strong sense of being a self and having a vocation, only in the hands of others and, finally, in the hands of God. These are difficult dispositions to cultivate, especially when the sharply felt expectations of a particular church form the immediate setting for our vocation. Nonetheless, we must resolutely remind ourselves that the Body of Christ is always larger than the members at hand and that the corporate support for our leadership may come from members far away in time and space.

We can see some of this in the story of a minister who was tempted not to lead on matters of sexual violence. He was the pastor of a large suburban church. A friend of his working in their church's national office invited him to attend a series of workshops on sexual and domestic violence that her board was about to offer in his area. He was happy to speak with her but assured her that in the four years he had been at his church, he had never heard even a rumor about such problems in the congregation. He wasn't sure how people would react if he took part in the workshops. It might cause a scandal if some people assumed his participation meant he suspected church members of being involved in spouse abuse or incest. His people weren't comfortable talking about such things, and since the issues hadn't come up, why rock the boat? He thanked her for her good work with people who needed such assistance.

His friend, however, wouldn't give up. She called him back right before the workshop and pointed out that the national incidence of sexual violence made it likely that if he didn't have the problem in his present church, he would probably run into it in the future. He said when that happened he'd get back in touch with her for help; she replied that might be too late for him to minister effectively on the spot. Finally she appealed to their friendship, asking him to attend the workshops for her sake, out of support for her ministry in organizing them.

This personal appeal worked at last. Because he had been late in acting, he had to withdraw from a youth group meeting he had planned to attend the night of the first workshop. On the Sunday before, during announcements from the pulpit, he apologized for missing the meeting, saying he was going to attend a minister's workshop called "Responding to Sexual and Domestic Violence." He arrived at the Thursday workshop a shaken man. Five church members from different families had contacted him so far that week, tearfully letting him know of situations of abuse, some of which had been going on long before he arrived in the church. When he asked them why they had not come to him sooner, they all said he had made them feel he was not willing to discuss such disturbing matters until he announced he was going to the workshop.

During that difficult week and the weeks to come, the pastor realized that by not admitting he had a hard time facing sexual violence personally, he had withheld leadership in his church from those who desperately needed it. His experience not only enabled him to overcome his complacency, pride, and fear but also taught him that where he could not lead on his own, there were others he could rely on if he admitted he needed the help. Finally, he came to realize that he had allowed what he saw as the expectations of his congregation to reinforce his temptation not to lead. It might well have been true that many people would be upset if he exercised leadership on such a controversial matter. But in fact it did turn out to be true that others were dying for lack of such leadership. By relying too much on his own reading of the congregation, he had become a prisoner of the status quo and of his own deep-seated fears. It was only through the support and presence of other people that he found a renewed sense of authority to act out of his vocation to love and serve God and neighbor.[15]

We are not the authors of the stories of the good that draw our hearts to God. We need to realize that our entanglement in the accidents of history will never end. The conflicting expectations placed on us can never be met. We will always be tempted by complacency, pride, and fears not to exercise that transforming leadership that is always risky yet finally necessary to move to the destination of our hearts. The power to move through entanglement and fear comes only from our faith that in this risky business we have the support and presence of the Body of Christ and the freedom of our calling to lead without counting the cost in failure or success.

We began this chapter looking at the web of entanglement Paul got himself into in Corinth, and at the troubles that beset him in his exercise of leadership. Paul showed a great capacity for learning from experience. We have already seen this in the markedly different tone he took in his second plea to the Corinthians on behalf of the collection. We can see it also in Paul's swift reaction to new information about the situation in Corinth. If we are to resist the complacency, pride, and fears that tempt us not to lead, we too must be open to new voices and new perspectives, to the support and presence of others in our leadership.

Yet in doing this there is finally no substitute for our personal presence. In his struggles in Corinth, Paul's very absence and the letters he sent in his place became divisive issues that gave credence to the arguments of those who challenged Paul's leadership, forcing Paul to respond: "Someone said, 'His letters are weighty enough, and full of strength, but when you see him in person, he makes no impression and his powers of speaking are negligible.' I should like that sort of person to take note that our deeds when we are present will show the same qualities as our letters when we are at a distance" (II Cor. 10:10-11).

The leader must remain on the edge in order to lead, as I have argued in earlier chapters. But the leader must also have an active presence within the community in order to claim solidarity with it. This presence need not always be physical, as the continuing importance of the imprisoned and isolated Nelson Mandela proves abundantly. But a leader who is physically absent and whose presence is sustained by letters, books, or fellow workers must constantly strive to make that presence powerful and real. Paul's visits, fellow workers, and many letters may have finally established the authority of his presence, and the presence of his authority, among the Christians at Corinth. But without that sense of embodied presence in the community, Paul or any other leader risks going so far off the edge as to become unconnected with the center, thereby losing the credibility that gives the leader's voice the power to move the center to begin with. Although leaders must admit their need for the support and presence of others, they must be willing to extravagantly give their support and presence in return, for that willingness itself marks them as leaders.

Paul's experience also reminds us that the risks of living on the edge, of leading toward a vision you yourself may have only seen through a glass darkly, raises fears and misgivings that themselves pose serious threats to the exercise of leadership. Paul puts a good face on his own quick exit and subsequent withdrawal from a personal confrontation at Corinth. "I made up my mind, then, that my next visit to you would not be a painful one, for if I cause you distress I am causing distress to my only possible source of joy" (II Cor. 2:1). "If anyone did cause distress, he caused it not to me, but—not to exaggerate—in some degree to all of you" (II Cor. 2:5). Although Paul wants to express solidarity with the Corinthians' pain, linking it with his own, that does not make his any less painful. "Indeed, I wrote as I did precisely to spare myself distress when I visited you. . . . I wrote to you in agony of mind" (II Cor. 2:3-4). These painful feelings may well have affected his leadership during his emergency visit and his subsequent "tearful letter." How he responded to them certainly became an issue, not only for him personally but also for the success of his leadership in Corinth.[16]

Paul's tangled relationship with the particular community he sought to lead, and the fears that beset him in doing so, appear in a poignant way later in II Corinthians. After defending the integrity and trustworthiness of his ministry and before summarizing his argument and appealing for the collection, Paul writes the following:

> I can speak with the greatest frankness to you; and I can speak with the greatest pride about you: in all our hardship, I am filled with encouragement and overflowing with joy. Even after we had come to Macedonia, there was no rest for this body of ours. Far from it; we were beset by hardship on all sides, there were quarrels all around us and misgivings within us. But God, who encourages all those who are distressed, encouraged us through the arrival of Titus; and not simply by his arrival only, but also by means of the encouragement that you had given him, as he told us of your desire to see us, how sorry you were and how concerned for us; so that I was all the more joyful. (II Cor. 7:4-7)

Paul, one suspects, always spoke frankly and was equally capable of being filled with pride, pain, and joy. All three are present here, and all are bound up in his relationship with the Corinthians. But more than that, his ministry with them is itself bound up with God and driven by the love of God and neighbor. He is therefore capable of taking pride and joy in the same relationship that causes him pain. Paul goes to great lengths to emphasize that it is not just the arrival of a friend that brings him joy but the news Titus brings about transformations in the Corinthian church. This was news, incomplete as it turned out, of the apparent success of Paul's tearful letter in bringing about repentance and change in the community. More than that, it was news of the continued viability of Paul's relationship with the Corinthian church. Paul's fears had not only been for the failure of his leadership but also for what that implied about his relationship to that community, a relationship that rested on their common membership in the Body of Christ. This connection had been in view from the start of his letter: "For just as the sufferings of Christ overflow into our lives, so too does the encouragement we receive through Christ" (II Cor. 1:5).

Paul countered threats without and threats within by holding fast to the story of Christ and tried in his letters and visits to make this story come alive for the Corinthians. In this he may have been only partly successful. The most we can say is that what success he had took place in fits and starts over a long period of time. But that should be perfectly normal and nothing to be wondered at, for lasting transformation is like that in this world. In the entangled networks of relationships where leadership takes place and in the conflicted hearts of those who lead and follow, such imperfect and gradual success is only to be expected, yet nothing to prevent us from trying. And that, perhaps, is the real lesson we learn from Paul when we face the temptation not to lead.

CHAPTER 6

THE TEMPTATION TO BETRAY

Paul's turbulent relationship with the Christians at Corinth still has much to tell us about the complexities of moral leadership. We have seen Paul telling the story in the center, appealing to the Corinthians for solidarity with other Christian communities. We have seen him entangled in the accidents of history, trying to keep a presence in the Corinthian community while traveling far out on its edge. But Paul also faced in Corinth an additional challenge no less dangerous in our day than in his. In his opposition to the "super-apostles," we can hear him calling the community back to the story of Christ that it had been tempted to betray. Here we can begin to ponder the temptation, afflicting leaders and followers alike, to betray the story of the good that has claimed their hearts.

Several times in the Corinthian correspondence,[1] Paul refers to other missionary figures who seem to have been active in Corinth, preaching a gospel at odds with Paul's story of Christ.[2] At first glance the opposition seems merely personal, something that Paul meets by refuting the charges of his opponents. Whereas these rival missionaries offer letters of recommendation attesting to the worthiness of their preaching,[3] Paul tells the Corinthians their own character is the surest proof of the power of Paul's preaching. "You yourselves are our letter, written in our hearts, that everyone can read and understand" (II Cor. 3:2). His opponents seem to have accepted wages for their preaching and may have accused Paul of shaming the Corinthians in rejecting financial support.[4] In reply Paul asks, "Have I done wrong, then, humbling myself so that you might be raised up, by preaching the Gospel of God to you for nothing?" (II Cor. 11:7).

Finally, his opponents seem to have relied on an impressive demonstration of spiritual gifts and religious experiences as evidence of their superior authority.[5] Paul rejects this charge of spiritual inferiority in no uncertain terms. "Now, I consider that I am not in the least inferior to the super-apostles. Even if there is something lacking in my public speaking, this is not the case with my knowledge, as we have openly shown to you at all times and before everyone" (II Cor. 11:5-6). Paul goes to great lengths to demonstrate this claim. "Whatever bold claims anyone makes—now I am talking as a fool—I can make them too" (II Cor. 11:21). "I have turned into a fool, but you forced me to it. It is you that should have been commending me; those super-apostles had no advantage over me, even if I am nothing at all" (II Cor. 12:11).

Paul boasts as a "fool" because he refuses to be misled into merely defending himself. He knows that more is at stake here than his personal style of leadership. The controversy concerns the story of Christ itself, and the manner of telling the story that most truthfully embodies it. For what fundamentally threatened Paul's leadership was the potential these rival missionaries carried with them for the betrayal of the story Paul had entrusted to the Corinthians. More than a difference in missionary style, they represented a different interpretation of the story of Jesus and a different model for the journey of the Christian life. Paul recognized these high stakes very clearly when he chides the Corinthians:

> But I am afraid that, just as the snake with his cunning seduced Eve, your minds may be led astray from single-minded devotion to Christ. Because any chance comer has only to preach a Jesus other than the one we preached, or you have only to receive a spirit different from the one you received, or a gospel different from the one you accepted—and you put up with that only too willingly. (II Cor. 11:3-4)

At the root of the conflict, Paul sees that the Corinthians are being tempted to betray the story of Christ that he and his fellow-workers had entrusted to them. That is why we have seen him moving to overcome this temptation by asserting not just his right to tell the story of Christ but his authority over against others to interpret it for the community, and the responsibility of the Corinthians to hold on to the story they had received.[6] In doing this Paul appeals to the Corinthians' fondness for religious experience by asking them to consider their own lives as evidence of the presence of Christ, just as he has offered stories of his own life as proof to them. The test of faith is not in letters of commendation or exotic signs and wonders but in the very presence of Christ shaping our lives. "Put yourself to the test to make sure you are in the faith. Examine yourselves. Do you not recognize yourselves as people in whom Jesus Christ is present?—unless, that is, you fail the test. But we, as I hope you will come to recognise, do not fail the test" (II Cor. 13:5-6).

This is not what we would think of today as a doctrinal test. In fact, we know little about the substance of what Paul's opponents were saying to tempt the Corinthians. It was—and is today—a test of vision and character. Have we seen rightly the vision pictured in the story of Christ? Have we let that vision become the guiding force in shaping who we are and who we are becoming? Paul condemns his opponents not just for their divergent missionary style. He also asserts that people who need letters of commendation setting them apart as somehow special, or who demand payment for preaching the good news of the gospel, or who revel in personal experiences and boast in spiritual deeds—those people and the ones who follow them have so narrowed or twisted the story of Christ as to misunderstand it completely.

The story of Christ tells of one who was rejected by the world rather than given letters of commendation; who refused to lord it over others rather than charge them for services; who became weak that others might become strong. The story of Christ gives Paul confidence in rejecting the claims of the super-apostles, for in its light they betray themselves by their own conduct.[7] "These people are counterfeit apostles, dishonest workers disguising themselves as apostles of Christ" (II Cor. 11:13).

That same story gives him confidence in calling the Corinthians back to faithfulness and obedience, for Paul's very concern for their fidelity to God's word carries with it the proof of his own authority. "All this time you have been thinking that we have been pleading our own cause before you; no, we have been speaking in Christ and in the presence of God—and all, dear friends, to build you up" (II Cor. 12:19). Even the threat of harshness is tempered by Paul's conformity to the story of Christ.

> We have no power to resist the truth; only to further the truth; and we are delighted to be weak only if you are strong. What we ask in our prayers is that you should be made perfect. That is why I am writing this while still far away, so that when I am with you I shall not have to be harsh, with the authority that the Lord has given me, an authority that is for building up and not for breaking down. (II Cor. 13:8-10)

Paul claims authority because, in contrast to his opponents, he follows the example of Christ, who was weak so that others could be strong. Nonetheless, he assures the Corinthians he will be strong if he has to be, in order that they might be made perfect, as God desires them to become. As one commentator observes, "Whether the paradox impressed his original readers as much as it has modern theologians, we cannot be sure."[8] Paradoxical or not, Paul was insisting that his opponents betrayed the gospel not just by their doctrinal message but in the self-important conduct of their ministry. In addition, he was maintaining that the Corinthians betrayed the gospel in their willingness to follow false apostles who told a more exotic version of the story they had heard from Paul.

Paul's own experience of the temptation to betray a story by pursuing its goals with inappropriate means is demonstrated both by Paul's own recognition of the foolishness of his boasting ("I shall not be following the Lord's way in what I say now"—II Cor. 11:17) and by his reluctance to resort to the harsh imposition of authority ("Yes, my appeal to you is that I should not have to be bold when I am actually with you"—II Cor. 10:2).

The stories of leadership and vocation we have been

following thus far depict people struggling with moral leadership and fighting the temptation not to lead. In order to find examples of true betrayal and to see moral leadership in opposition to it, we will need to go farther afield. We will encounter people tempted to betray by refusing to hear the stories and see the reality of the people around them. We will meet people locked in betrayal, twisting stories and lives in an attempt to justify their abandonment of the story of Christ.

Stories of genuine betrayal may seem distant from us, but they are closer than we want to think, as close as our yielding to the small voice that says moral leadership is someone else's task. As we shall have occasion to ponder in what lies ahead, it is a fearful thing to do as Paul asks and put ourselves to the test, but there is, finally, no other path to our destination.

Refusing to Hear and to See

I have spoken before of the rich complexity found in stories of the good, and of the many voices that go together over the years to tell that story from one generation to the next. As we saw in chapter 4, one of the most demanding tasks of transforming leadership is the challenge to hear new voices and tell new stories. We need to consider now what occurs in the absence of this hearing, in the refusal to hear voices and see new visions opening up before us. It is possible to *think* we are listening and looking, even while we listen without hearing and look without seeing what is there. A refusal to see and to hear does more than complicate transforming leadership. It can put those who persist in it well on the path toward betraying their story, their community, and themselves.

Earlier we observed the temptation not to lead as it affected Linda's community in the selection of a new campus minister. In their search they ran across the story of another, quite different selection process that made them feel fortunate for their own, with all its imperfections. The campus ministry at this other university had begun as an outreach of the local Roman Catholic diocese. Over many years of effective leadership under the same director, the ministry had grown tremendously and had formed close ties with other denominational ministries operating out of the central Campus Ministry Office. The ministry was staffed by the director, an associate director who was a Roman Catholic nun, and several part-time assistants, both religious and lay. After his long tenure, the priest who had been the director decided to retire. He notified his superiors of this, and they told him they would begin the process of selecting a successor. He also notified the rest of the staff and the central Campus Ministry office. The staff offered their congratulations on his impending retirement and promised their assistance in choosing a successor. The head of the central office also sent his congratulations and wrote to the diocesan superiors indicating his willingness to help in the upcoming search. He received a reply thanking him for his offer.

Nothing happened for several months, at least nothing in the public eye. Suddenly an announcement was made from the diocesan offices, noting the appointment of a new director. The community was thrown into great confusion. No one knew or had heard of the person named as director. Everyone thought the search had been suspended or delayed for some reason. When questioned, the retiring director revealed he had attended a private meeting with diocesan officials, at which two members of the community invited by the diocese were also present. The central Campus Ministry office had not been invited to send a representative. This meeting had apparently served as the search, for soon afterward the new director had been appointed.

The community's confusion turned to anger when the new director, without consulting community members about their needs or even visiting the campus, sent word that the services of the associate minister and one of the assistants would no longer be needed, and they were given notice to leave before the start of the next term. Having first felt it was being ignored, the community now felt it was being trifled with. Many members felt that the associate director was being dismissed because she was a woman, whose presence threatened the new director. Others felt the assistant was being dismissed because he was not a local priest and because he had often allowed the associate director to share the pulpit in a conversational sermon. In the absence of any public discussion, such speculation about the new director's motives flourished unchecked. In any case, people asked how someone who had never been in the community could know its needs, or the events over the years out of which the present structures of ministry had evolved. Many community members wrote letters of complaint to the diocese, voicing their exasperation along with their concern that the new director's leadership would be compromised before it began by the method of his selection and his subsequent treatment of the current staff. Their pleas fell on seemingly deaf ears, and by the time Linda's friends had heard the story, there were no prospects for change in the situation that had been imposed on the community.

The community in this story certainly felt betrayed, but how, and by whom? From the perspective of the church hierarchy, no betrayal had occurred because standard procedures had been followed. A church job had been filled by church officials with the consultation of the previous occupant of the position and two members of the community. From the perspective of the new director, no betrayal had occurred because he was operating within his prerogatives, deciding on the staff he wanted to work with. Yet the community members were distraught, feeling they could no longer trust leaders who failed to listen to them and wondering about their future as a church community. They experienced the situation as a betrayal *by* church officials and the new director and a betrayal *of* their community and the larger story of what it meant to become the church community toward which they had been moving for many years.

Whether the church officials and the new director would accept such a description or not, the situation from the point of view of the community certainly is one of power-wielding rather than leadership. As we have seen, transforming leadership seeks to incorporate the motives and resources of an entire community in order to move toward a common goal and puts the leader at risk in offering a vision of movement to the community. Transactional leadership seeks to broker shorter-term interests and needs according to the longer-term goals of the community. Neither form of leadership occurred here. Instead, only the needs and goals of the institutional church were taken into account, and no serious attempt was made to discern the needs, motives, and goals of the affected community. The church failed to hear the community's voice, and indications are that the new director will have a hard time hearing the voices of those in the community who do not already share his vision of the ministry. Failing to put himself at risk, he will most likely fail at transforming leadership. He will not be trusted to broker people's genuine interests and will likely fail at transactional leadership. The only recourse left to him, if he continues in the way he has begun, will be to call for obedience to the power he wields as an official representative of the institutional church. He will stand neither in the center nor on the edge but somewhere above the community, isolated from an effective relationship with it. Perhaps this worst-case scenario will not happen, but in any case, the new director and his church superiors face a difficult task in regaining the trust and cooperation of the community.

"Betrayal" may be more clearly recognized by those who feel betrayed than by those accused of betraying. One group may feel betrayed by others who feel they are the only true defenders of the story both groups share. Sometimes only time can tell which group kept the faith and which betrayed it. One thing we can say is that the path to betrayal begins with the refusal to hear the full range of voices whose interests are at stake in a given situation, where the direction of movement to be made is itself open to debate. This refusal to hear results in a narrowed telling of the story and more often than not will serve the interests of those already in positions of power and authority. Whether we refuse to hear out of a conviction of the rightness of our position or from a plain desire to wield power, our refusal makes it impossible to test the vision we pursue by subjecting it to the scrutiny of a richly complex telling of the story of the good. As a result, that story is no longer the generative matrix of a whole community but the fragile possession of those in control of how it is told.[9]

We saw something of this going on in the story of the legacy.

In one scenario, the pastor first revealed the legacy to a small group of the most powerful members of the community. They decided what to do with the unexpected gift before letting the wider community know about it and so presented it in such a way as to close off debate about other possible uses. Only a small fraction of the voices of the community was heard, and the movement that was made served the interests of those in powerful positions. These people were not official members of the institutional church, but their voices were obviously more important to the pastor than those of other community members, and this gave them an unofficial authority that allowed them to control the direction of the whole community on this matter. One suspects that group usually controls most of what goes on in such a community. Since this power-wielding is hidden to the public eye, the community may not even realize it is being manipulated, let alone have a focus for complaint or opposition.

In such a situation, any claims to moral leadership become false. The full range of vision of the story of the good is not being brought to bear on the formation of the community's character. Only certain voices are heard, certain visions seen—only those that tell the story in a way comforting to the people with the power to control its telling. Such a selective hearing and seeing is a form of what Walter Brueggemann has called "royal consciousness."[10] Leaders who practice it lust for power and possessions, whether material or symbolic, and seductively promise fulfillment to their obedient followers. By tightly controlling the story of the good, these "leaders" control the people as well. It is really false to call this leadership, because no leading is going on, or at the most only that which is closed rather than open to alternative interpretations of the past and the future.

This is why, as Brueggemann points out, the breaking of such control requires the loud voice of the prophet calling people back to the story of the good.[11] Moses speaking against the Pharaohs, Jeremiah against the kings of Judah, Second Isaiah against the narrow despair of the exile, Jesus against the trust in law and power and prestige, so tempting now as in his day—each of these transforming leaders spoke from the edge, breaking the false, ruling consciousness that had narrowed down the story to that which served the interests of the center.

The refusal to hear and to see begins in the temptation not to lead and ends in the temptation to betray. It is a refusal to admit the existence of the edge, a declaration that only the center's voice need be heard, only the center's vision seen. Initially this tempts us not to lead, or not to engage in the critical following moral leadership requires. But because other voices clamor to be heard and other visions present themselves from within the richness of the story of the good, sooner or later attempts to maintain this refusal require our active conspiracy against the voices of the edge. This sets us on the path to betrayal, for it suggests that we have access to God in a way our neighbor does not. Worse yet, it suggests we do not need to take our neighbors seriously, let alone struggle to love them, as we try to move forward on the journey toward God. This is surely the path to betrayal, for it pits each one against the other and, finally, all against the God revealed in Christ. I am not suggesting there is an easy way to separate one person's betrayal from another's fidelity. I am suggesting that a sure path to betrayal is the refusal to hear another person's charge of our *own* infidelity, or to see the story of Christ through the vision our neighbor offers to us. Much can be debated and much disputed, but the refusal to hear and see prevents any moral deliberation over the direction set by the powerful in our corporate journey toward the destination of the heart. In the resulting silence a betrayal begins whose consequences can be shattering indeed.

Twisting Stories and Lives

The temptation to betray finally twists the story of the good and leads its victims to do things that run counter to the real destination of the story in order to defend the twisted version. This is the end result of what happens when leaders and followers fail to resist the temptation not to lead and persist in refusing to hear dissenting voices. The community becomes further and further removed from the creative conflict that comes from listening to the guiding story in its complexity and to the diverse voices of the real world—of the center and the edge and communities beyond. As a result, those who follow and those who lead are no longer the kind of people envisioned by the story of the good, but something else masquerading in its name. Their lives are twisted, too.

It is almost too easy to come up with examples of such betrayal. We think of the gradual buildup of massive self-deception that culminated in Hitler's Germany,[12] or the apocalyptic collapse in the jungle of Jim Jones' People's Temple.[13] The extremity of these examples seems to let us off the hook, as we are tempted to say, "That can't happen here."

But betrayal also takes less obviously dramatic forms that hit quite closer to home. The student pastor trying to figure out how to respond to her friend, her senior pastor, and her church community was told by some earnest Christians that she should not help her friend because, after all, AIDS is God's punishment on homosexuals. The associate pastor at the social concerns meeting overheard people saying that the woman who sought support for a rally against capital punishment could not possibly be a Christian, because God demanded an eye for an eye. The pastor watching the well-capping knew he had church members who would justify capping the well by claiming that God put the mark of Cain on black people so that the offspring of Cain and Abel would not mix. Each twisted use of these biblical stories puts us farther along the path to betrayal. Far from being an extreme possibility that grabs spectacular headlines and only happens to people far removed in time and distance, the temptation to betray is as close to us as fear of the stranger. Perhaps this simply shows how radical the call to love the neighbor really is.

I want to focus on an example of betrayal that shows clearly how the story of the good is twisted and how lives are in consequence twisted too. The setting is South Africa, and the particular betrayal is summed up in the practice of apartheid. Let us not be lulled into thinking the South African situation is another one of those faraway examples that could not happen here. It already *has* happened here, and in many ways *continues* to happen, in the treatment of Native Americans, blacks, women, and a long list of those we see as dangerous strangers instead of welcome neighbors in whose face God shines.[14] We can learn much about our own land as we look at how those who lead the struggle against apartheid do so in the name of the God whose story apartheid shames. They stand for us, as we should stand with them, in defending the love of God and neighbor against a betrayal that twists stories and lives.

"Apartheid" is an Afrikaner word derived from the Dutch for "apartness," or the state of being separated from other concepts or things by being distinct and unique. More specifically, however, apartheid refers to the white South African practice of regulating society by rigid racial separation, to the advantage of the white minority population. Even as dispassionate a source as *Webster's Ninth New Collegiate Dictionary* gives the primary definition of apartheid as "racial segregation, *specif.:* a policy of segregation and political and economic discrimination against non-European groups in the Republic of So. Africa." As Desmond Tutu notes, the policy has been cloaked by other names, but "separate development" and "parallel democracy" still boil down to the racist concept of apartheid.[15]

Apartheid has been given various justifications by its practitioners, ranging from power politics—the right of white control based on historical Afrikaner dominance—to "cultural preservation"—the need to keep the cultural purity of white, Indian, and so-called "tribal" black Africans.[16] What concerns us most here, however, is the defense of apartheid on religious grounds. Although racism has been a problem at some time in most white South African churches,[17] we will focus on the dominant white Afrikaner Dutch Reformed Church, the Nederduitse Gereformeerde Kerk (NGK).

Religious life and relations between the races have had a rocky connection in South Africa for many years. A 1754 Dutch Reformed church ruling reflects local practice in preventing black Christians "from remaining in the foyer of the church after the church service."[18] From 1823 to 1829, a dispute arose over admitting black African converts to communion in heretofore all-white congregations. Through a fairly tortuous path of theological reasoning and political power-wielding,[19] this dispute continued into 1857, when it was resolved in what would be an ominous instance of twisting the Christian story and the people the story would form.

The NGK Synod of that year contains the following resolution:

> The Synod considers it desirable and according to Holy Scripture that our heathen members be accepted and initiated into our congregations wherever it is possible; but where this measure, as a result of the weakness of some, would stand in the way of promoting the work of Christ among the heathen people, then congregations set up among the heathen, or still to be set up, should enjoy their Christian privileges in a separate building or institution.[20]

By 1865 such a separate building was put up by the congregation of Zwartland, and by 1881 the separation had indeed been institutionalized with the founding of the Nederduitse Gereformeerde Sendingkerk (Dutch Reformed Mission Church) as a racially separate "black" church.[21] By 1948 the official newspaper of the NGK was able to say, "As a Church we have always worked purposefully for the separation of the races. In this regard apartheid can rightfully be called a church policy."[22] In 1975 an NGK minister, in a piece called *Credo of an Afrikaner,* is able to see apartheid as a linchpin of biblical morality whose embrace defines one as a Christian:

> I know of no other policy as moral, as responsible to Scripture, as the policy of separate development. . . . If the . . . Christian Afrikaner can be convinced there are no principles or biblical foundations for this policy of separate development, it is but a step to the conviction that it is un-Christian. And if we believe it is un-Christian or immoral it is our obligation to fight it.[23]

The religious defense of apartheid, begun as a missionary tool prompted by the weakness of some intolerant white Christians, has been twisted so far as to become a litmus test of adherence to a "Christian" story no longer open to conflicting voices. As another NGK official has put it: "Our only guide is the Bible. Our policy and outlook on life are based on the

Bible. We firmly believe the way we interpret it is right. We will not budge one inch from our interpretation to satisfy anyone in South Africa or abroad."[24]

Because it is a twisting of the Christian story, religious opposition to apartheid has included the reinterpretation of biblical texts used by the Afrikaners to support apartheid. In this regard the story of the Tower of Babel, Genesis 11:1-9, merits special attention. "Throughout the whole tradition of this NGK theology of race relations this has been in effect the cardinal text."[25] The story recounts the wandering of the descendants of Noah after the flood, at a time when "the whole world spoke the same language," and their settling in the valley of Shinar, where they determined to build a city.

> "Come," they said, "let us build ourselves a city and a tower with its top reaching heaven. Let us make a name for ourselves, so that we do not get scattered all over the world." Now Yahweh came down to see the city and the tower that the people had built. "So they are all a single people with a single language!" said Yahweh. "This is only the start of their undertakings! Now nothing they plan to do will be beyond them. Come, let us go down and confuse their language there, so that they cannot understand one another." Yahweh scattered them thence all over the world, and they stopped building the city. That is why it was called Babel, since there Yahweh confused the language of the whole world and from there Yahweh scattered them all over the world. (Gen. 11:4-9)

Immediately preceding this passage, in Genesis 10, is a long and detailed genealogy of the descendants of Noah's sons, intended to indicate the repopulating of the world after the flood and the wide range of human beings over the world. Frequent mention is made of this diversity of place and language: "These were Japheth's sons, in their respective countries, each with its own language, by clan and nation" (Gen. 10:5). Of the mighty Nimrod we are told that "the mainstays of his empire were Babel, Erech and Accad, all of them in the land of Shinar" (Gen. 10:10), and again of Ham's and Shem's descendants we are told they were divided "by clans and languages, by countries and nations" (of Ham, Gen. 10:20; of Shem, Gen. 10:31). The chapter ends "Such were the clans of Noah's descendants, listed by descent and nation. From them, other nations branched out on earth after the flood" (Gen. 10:32).

Why, then, does Genesis 11 tell the story of the Tower of Babel as if it were the *cause* of the spreading out of nations already detailed in Genesis 10? What we have is two traditions at work making two different but related theological points. Genesis 10 comes chiefly from the Priestly tradition, and it wants to affirm the unity of the human race in its diversity as an outcome of the divine blessing Noah received after the flood. Genesis 11 comes from the much earlier Yahwist tradition, which, emphasizing Yahweh's direct power and rule over the earth, explains the division into nations and the presence of many languages as a result of human pride and ambition, sins that alienate humans from God and from one another. In addition, the details of the story in Genesis 11 hint at the sin of idolatry, as the Tower of Babel is likely a reference to a ziggurat, or Babylonian temple, which would have been found on the plain of Shinar. The Hebrew Scriptures retain both traditions because each affirms something important about humankind's reliance on the power and righteousness of Yahweh.[26]

This quick sketch of the commonly accepted understanding of the Tower of Babel finds a sharp contrast in its twisted telling by those who see it as a justification for apartheid. Douglas Bax has provided a detailed analysis of the NGK interpretation of this text, as found in its 1976 report, *Human Relations and the South African Scene in the Light of Scripture*.[27] For the NGK, the people on the plain of Shinar sinned, not by their prideful construction of a tower to reach heaven but in their attempt to remain one people, undivided by language, race, and custom, in direct disobedience to (what the NGK understands as) God's command in Genesis 1:28, that humanity should divide into separate *volke* (peoples). God punishes these sinners by scattering them into races with different languages, thereby underscoring God's plan that each race should live separated from the others. Knowing that the Bible does not explicitly mention apartheid as a concrete doctrine, the NGK summarizes its conclusions thus:

> The diversity of races and peoples to which the confusion of tongues contributes is an aspect of reality which God obviously intended for this dispensation. To deny this fact is to side with the tower builders. Therefore a policy which in broad terms (as distinct from its concrete implementation) bears this reality in mind, is Biblically realistic in the good sense of the word. . . . [and thus] the policy of separate development retains . . . validity.[28]

Bax notes that this interpretation relies on a prior twisting of Genesis 1:28: "God blessed them, saying to them, 'Be fruitful, multiply, fill the earth and subdue it.'" Although this text is commonly understood to express God's blessing on human procreation and humankind's role as stewards of creation under God's rule, the NGK, standing at the center of a culture that survives by controlling other people, hears it saying that only by separating into different peoples or cultures can humankind carry out God's command to rule the earth. With this in mind, the tower builders are disobeying God in trying to be a single people, so that God further scatters humankind into races that must be kept separate, each holding to its own territory, language, and culture. Bax observes that the NGK reads back into the texts the divided state of race relations in South Africa: "As the [NGK] Report in many places makes clear, it really attempts to argue from what *is* to what *ought to be*, i.e., from the observed fact of diverse *volke* and races in mankind to the conclusion that God must will that we maintain this diversity by keeping the races separate."[29]

Bax points out that the NGK locates the sin of the tower builders in Genesis 11:1, "The whole world spoke the same language," rather than 11:4, "'Come,' they said, 'let us build ourselves a city and a tower with its top reaching heaven. Let us make a name for ourselves, so that we do not get scattered all over the world.'" The unity of humanity is original and provided by God (just as we saw the diversity explained by the Priestly tradition as also provided by God). In fact, it is the attempt to preserve that unity by *human* means apart from God that, I have already noted, distinguishes Genesis 11 from Genesis 10. It is pride, ambition, and idolatry that Yahweh punishes in Genesis 11, exactly the sort of pride that the defenders of apartheid display in striving to keep *themselves* a separate, single people. As Bax maintains,

> Thus the story of Babel in fact directly and radically *opposes* the Report's attempt to make so much of cultural identity and achievement. Indeed the text warns that it is precisely an attempt like that of the Afrikaner *volke* to secure its own future as a *volke* or nation by attempting to secure its cultural identity from the threat of finitude or eventual dissolution that brings upon itself the judgment of God and disaster, because it is a titanism that seeks security in that which is its own . . . , instead of in God alone.[30]

Bax goes on to analyze the NGK use of other passages from the Old and New testaments, each one dependent on and more willfully bizarre than the last. None is perhaps more ironic than the twisting even of the work of Christ and the coming of the Spirit in the NGK reading of the miracle at Pentecost (Acts 2:5-11). With such a commitment not to hear any voices on the edge of their narrow center, the Afrikaners become unable to hear the voice of Scripture, even when voices are at issue. The miracle of the tongues, when the power of the Word restores the unity of language lost at the Tower of Babel by making it possible for people assembled from many lands and languages to understand the preaching of Peter, somehow becomes an affirmation of "separate development" because it "confirms that it is the will of God that each man should learn of the great deeds of God in his own language."[31] Far to the contrary, Bax declares, "What Pentecost means, therefore, is that the gift of the Spirit at Jerusalem together with the proclamation of the Gospel reverses the centrifugal force of the curse of Babel. For the Spirit unites us into the *one* people of God, the one *body* of Christ."[32]

Moral leadership in opposition to apartheid also proceeds by condemning it as a heretical betrayal of Christian tradition, and, more specifically, of the Reformed or Calvinist tradition. Such a charge accuses the defenders of apartheid not only of twisting specific biblical stories but also of an obdurate self-deception on a grander scale. Alan Boesak has been particularly identified with this opposition through his activities in South Africa, his leadership within the World Alliance of Reformed Churches (WARC), and his international publications, which include essays, addresses, and sermons delivered inside South Africa as well as worldwide.[33]

Of Boesak's many essays and speeches I will focus on two that most clearly present the argument for condemning apartheid as a betrayal of Reformed Christian tradition. "Black and Reformed: Contradiction or Challenge?" was first presented at a conference of the Alliance of Black Reformed Christians in South Africa (ABRECSA) in October, 1981.[34] "God Made us All, But . . . Racism and the World Alliance of Reformed Churches," delivered at the WARC meeting in Ottowa, Canada, in 1982, helped move the WARC toward its official decision in the fall of that year to declare apartheid a heresy and to suspend communion with the NGK and allied churches that failed to reject apartheid.[35]

Boesak wants to claim the Reformed heritage as his own and make it accessible to black and white South Africans today. To do so he must argue against the use of the tradition by the NGK and allied white Dutch Reformed churches. Boesak wants to use the Reformed tradition to reform the Dutch Reformed, in much the same way Calvin sought to reform the church of his own time. He proceeds by noting important points where Dutch Reformed practice has sharply deviated from the wider Reformed tradition.

The supremacy of the word of God. The twisting described above holds the Scriptures hostage to human selection rather than allowing the full biblical message to open human hearts to the liberating voice of God. Such a narrow, human-controlled reading of Scripture is in direct opposition to the Reformed tradition, which based its own opposition to the church of its day on the principle of submission to the word of God alone. "Manipulation of the word of God to suit culture, prejudices, or ideology is alien to the Reformed tradition."[36]

The Lordship of Jesus Christ over the whole world. Boesak claims the NGK has twisted this basic Reformed premise into a demand for obedience to official authority. In contrast, he finds in it the promise that Christ redeems all aspects of human life and *is* the life of the world. As the people who worship this

Lord, Christians have the responsibility to see that all creation reflects the kingdom of God. "The exercise of that responsibility is part of the discipleship to which the Lord Jesus Christ has called us. It is not an addition to this discipleship, but an integral part of it. Doing what we can to reform the social world in which we live is part of our spiritual life.[37]

The brokenness of the world. Reformed doctrines of the sinfulness of humanity and the consequent brokenness of the world have been used by the Dutch Reformed to justify the status quo, as if continued fragmentation were God's will. They miss the humbling point that human sinfulness means human institutions will be "tainted by sin" and thus require constant reformation.

> In true Reformed theology . . . we understand that human beings do not automatically seek the glory of God and the good of their neighbor. That is why it becomes a Christian's task to work actively for the good of the neighbor. . . . This means that Reformed Christians are called on not to accept the sinful realities of the world. Rather we are called to challenge, to shape, to subvert, and to humanize history until it conforms to the norm of the kingdom of God.[38]

Boesak goes on to cite support for his argument from creedal statements and theologians in the Reformed tradition, including John Calvin, the Heidelberg Catechism, the Scottish Confession, Abraham Kuyper, and Karl Barth, as well as Beyers Naude (a contemporary white South African opponent of apartheid) and the statements of the black Dutch Reformed Mission Church.[39] On social justice, he finds Karl Barth supporting the edge of liberation against the center of retrenchment: "God always takes his stand unconditionally and passionately on this side and this side alone: against the lofty and on behalf of the lowly; against those who already enjoy right and privilege and on behalf of those who are denied and deprived of it."[40] On duty to the government, he finds no less a Reformer than John Calvin demanding obedience to official authority *only* when that authority itself is submissive to the word of God:

But in that obedience which we have shown to be due to the authority of rulers, we are always to make this exception, indeed to observe it as primary, that such obedience is never to lead us away from obedience to him to whose will the desires of all kings ought to be subject. . . . We have been redeemed by Christ at so great a price as our redemption cost him, so that we should not enslave ourselves to the wicked desire of men—much less be subject to their impiety.[41]

Boesak ends his ABRECSA address by noting the great spiritual strength and comfort that comes from declaring, "I, with body and soul, both in life and death, am not my own, but belong unto my faithful Savior, who is Jesus the Liberator, Christ the Messiah and *Kyrios,* the Lord."[42]

Such dedication carries over into his address to the World Alliance of Reformed Churches urging the declaration of apartheid as a heresy. Building on the theological rejection of apartheid as a betrayal of the Reformed tradition, he calls on the WARC to institutionalize that rejection on an international scale. Pointing to the particular responsibility of the Reformed churches in denouncing this heretical betrayal, he observes:

All this is of singular importance, for the struggle in South Africa is not merely against an evil ideology; it is against a pseudo-religious ideology that was born in and continues to be justified out of the bosom of the Reformed churches. The consequences of this for the future of the Christian church in South Africa are staggering, for ultimately, beyond denomination and tradition, the credibility of the gospel of Jesus Christ is at stake.[43]

Boesak goes on to denounce apartheid as a racist ideology that amounts to institutionalized sinfulness. This is because such racism is "not merely attitudinal, but structural."[44] It is a system of domination, imposed from without, that "denies the truth that all human beings are made in the image of the God and Father of Jesus Christ."[45] As such it is a form of idolatry that has "not only contaminated human society; it has also defiled the very body of Christ."[46] And, as Boesak grimly remarks, Christians must take a unified stand in rejecting this idolatry, because through the Dutch Reformed twisting of the Reformed tradition, "It is Christians who have provided the moral and theological justification for racism and human degradation."[47]

Finally, Boesak again turns to Calvin in making what proved to be his successful appeal to the WARC. Speaking of the Lord's Supper (a communion that apartheid makes virtually impossible for blacks and whites to share), Calvin said:

> Now since [Christ] has only one body, of which he makes us all partakers, it is necessary that all of us also be made one body by such participation. . . . We shall benefit very much from the Sacrament if this thought is impressed and engraved upon our minds: that none of the brethren can be injured, despised, rejected, abused, or in any kind offended by us, without at the same time, injuring, despising, and abusing Christ by the wrongs we do.[48]

Yielding to the temptation to betray looses an assault on the character of people whose hearts have been claimed by the story that is betrayed. The more the story is twisted, the more distorted its people and the world they live in become, and the higher the price exacted on the community and those around them to maintain the distorted vision, even to the price of a person's life. How tragically ironic that such killing is being done in South Africa in the name of Jesus Christ, who died so that others might live.

Moral leadership in opposition to apartheid thus reveals it as a clear betrayal of the Christian story. Apartheid is a structured destruction of the unity of the Body of Christ, a policy *against* instead of *for* the love of God and neighbor. There is room for debate, as the very necessity for arguing against apartheid illustrates, whether people involved in this naked power-wielding still think they are doing so in the service of a story of the good. But that is precisely where, as we have seen in earlier chapters, the possibility of transformation arises in the consciousness of conflict. In looking at the struggle in South Africa, we experience a reality that *can* happen wherever people refuse to hear the voices of dissent. The Dutch Reformed, and all those who so betray, persist in the face of moral opposition that claims that they so twist the story of the good as to make its ends unrecognizable in its pursuit, and that in doing so they also twist the lives of people subject to their domination. Their persistence in this betrayal is a measure of a fear of the stranger to which we no less than they are subject, and against which we must marshal the strength of the love of God and neighbor.

In 1983 Alan Boesak preached a sermon in Amsterdam in which he spoke of God's willingness to "start over again" with humanity despite our frequent betrayals, and of our need to be willing to start over again to live out God's love even in the face of suffering, betrayal, and death. Boesak's 1983 words speak a telling message to all who would resist in themselves and in others the temptation to betray: "If God wishes to start all over again with us in the resurrection of Jesus, that is God's insurrection against evil, disobedience, violence, murder—against sin. In 1983, in Jesus Christ, our story can be transformed and converted so that in the final analysis it is evident as the human story, the story that ends as God planned it to end."[49]

When we oppose apartheid, as in every case where we resist the temptation to betray and oppose those who have betrayed, we strive to become ever more worthy of the image of God we bear, so that we may glorify rather than shame the story of Christ that God tells through us in this place and time. Our call to a vocation of moral leadership demands no more and no less.

Testing and Temptation

Earlier in this chapter we heard Paul urging the Corinthians to put themselves to the test, a test of whether they found the presence of Christ among them in who they were and how they lived. We have since seen the many dangers of such testing and the consequences of failure, when we are tempted to narrow and twist the story to what *we* want "the presence of Christ" to mean. Paul's words take on a harsh and almost self-righteous tone. After all, don't we pray *not* to be led into temptation? Isn't it risky to demand that we test whether or not our hearts hold fast to the gospel?

Paul is suggesting that we can resist the temptation to betray only when we ask whether our lives faithfully reflect the character of God, whose story we find in the life, death, and resurrection of Jesus. Leaders and followers, super-apostles and everyday Corinthians, even Paul and Titus and their fellow workers, all must test themselves against the character of God revealed in the gentleness and kindness of Christ.

The temptation to betray appears as a willingness to narrow or twist the story of the good in order to meet one's own goals instead of the goals envisioned in the story. It appears as the willingness to follow rival storytellers when their story of the good is more congenial and less disruptive than the story to which we have been faithful. It appears as the willingness to put success above fidelity and to risk mixing inappropriate or dangerous means and ends in order to "succeed." The temptation to betray afflicts leaders and followers alike. Resisting the temptation is itself a form of testing, a way of checking whether our character is being formed by the character of the God revealed in Christ.

As we try to lead and to follow in our pursuit of the Christian life, we will do well to keep in mind the closing lines of Paul's surviving correspondence with that difficult Corinthian community. There Paul reminds us of our most effective resource in the personal and communal struggle against the temptation to betray.

> To end then, brothers, we wish you joy; try to grow perfect; encourage one another; have a common mind and live in peace, and the God of love and peace will be with you.
> Greet one another with the holy kiss. All God's holy people send you their greetings.
> The grace of the Lord Jesus Christ, the love of God and the fellowship of the Holy Spirit be with you all. (II Cor. 13:11-13)

This is the test Paul asks his sisters and brothers to pass today, a continual testing that proves strong against the temptation to betray. Only a reminder of the common destination of our hearts in the love of God and neighbor and the assurance of God's presence as we make our way there can keep leaders and followers from succumbing to the temptation to betray. That love which unites leaders and followers makes us bold to call upon God to make us strong when we are weak. It reminds us that God, not humankind, is the author of our story of the good. We hold fast to that story not alone but in community, and in the presence of God's love calling us forward. It is, after all, with confidence in such love, and in the assurance that we are people who do find God's presence in who we are and who we are becoming, that we say, in the words our Lord gave us, "Lead *us* not into temptation." Making the Lord's Prayer our own, we find the power to move on together.

CHAPTER 7

LIVING ON THE EDGE

In the preceding pages we have explored the call to ministry as a vocation of moral leadership in community. We have seen that call set those who answer it on a rich but perilous journey, trying to move themselves and others toward the destination of their hearts. Trying to be a moral leader is often a demoralizing task. Those who seek to lead find themselves enmeshed in the accidents of history of local communities. They can spend their energies in striving for status in the social structures of the church or struggle in the web of cultural expectations that circumscribe their profession and their power. They find themselves held down by people anxious to defend the status quo. Yet they also find themselves sustained by the call itself, nourished by inherited images of the minister and the stories of others who have led in God's name and buoyed up by critical followers often several steps ahead of their leaders on the path to the greater love of God and neighbor.

I have argued that the best perspective for the minister as moral leader is discovered in living on the edge rather than in the center of our communities. We have seen some of the dangers encountered in trying to be a moral leader, living a life on the edge. Leaders can be afflicted with complacency and pride. They can be tortured by fears of change, conflict, success, failure, disapproval, and isolation. They can be wracked with self-doubt and blinded by self-deception. They can be tempted to renounce leadership altogether, or to betray the story of the good that gave direction to their hearts.

Such difficulties beset all leaders. The *minister* as moral leader has a particular problem beyond these afflictions, an additional twist to the tension of life on the edge. Religious communities, whether local congregations or international churches, often put their ministers in a paralyzing bind by sending them double messages that can hardly be documented but that most any experienced minister has received. Go and lead the people, ministers are told, but not too fast. Transform the world for Christ, but not too far. Speak out against injustice, but be loyal to the structures of the church. Be creative in your preaching and teaching, but let the authorities limit what you have to say. This double message can be as blunt as the official silencing of a liberation theologian or as subtle as the "words of wisdom" addressed by a senior pastor to a minister fresh from seminary that "No one ever got to the pulpit of a high-steeple church in this district by preaching about the problems of the homeless."

That double bind is part of the pull to the center, and all the more reason for the minister as moral leader to try to live on the edge. For the antidote to the myopic vision of the center is the clarifying perspective of the edge. Remaining aware of other visions, other stories of the good, other voices telling the center's own story, we are released from the idolatry of following one human community's perspective as if it were God's own. That the world might be other than it is now is the critical insight of leadership, which comes from and generates true movement. Against this risky opportunity of transformation, the center offers only the desperate satisfaction of the status quo.

Yet as we have noted before, the edge and the center are bound inextricably together. Human communities *have* centers and edges as they delineate the boundaries of common stories of the good. The edge *is* the edge only of some center, and all centers require edges for their own definition. If edges and centers were not part of the complex telling of a common story, they would have nothing to offer and nothing to fear from each other.

The minister as moral leader must live on the edge but remain connected to the center. I have used the image of the minister "suspended" between center and edge to describe this peculiar position. By saying the minister must live on the edge, I mean that taking up life foursquare in the center collapses the tension that keeps the minister suspended. Life in the center is far too rewarding to keep us on the journey without conscious attention to movement on the edge. It is too tempting to sit safely in the privileged center of most Christian communities and find ourselves responding to the urgent voices of the edge by paraphrasing the distressingly ancient prayer, "Make me a Christian, Lord, but not yet."

The minister as moral leader, then, is something of a subversive. Dependent on the resources of the center, she must nonetheless remain ever critical of the story as the center tells it, alive to other voices on the edge. Dedicated to the service of the church, he must nonetheless remember his calling to serve God and neighbor first and question whether the church presently serves that overriding purpose. Sustained by the stories of ancestors in the faith, the minister must take up the constant struggle of interpreting and retelling those stories today. It is not enough for the minister as moral leader to be a mere storyteller. Alive on the edge, he or she must listen to many stories, interpret them in the light of the story of the heart, and retell them in a way to move the people of God to become the kind of people God is calling them to become.

Toward the end of one of the chronologically latest entries in the writings that became the Christian Scriptures, we get a glimpse of the venerable occupation of wrestling with stories of the servants of God. Speaking of the necessity of living holy lives in anticipation of the coming of our Lord, the author of II Peter appeals to Paul for support.[1]

> Our brother Paul, who is so dear to us, told you this when he wrote to you with the wisdom that he was given. He makes this point too in his letters as a whole wherever he touches on these things. In all his letters there are of course some passages which are hard to understand, and these are the ones that uneducated and unbalanced people distort, in the same way as they distort the rest of scripture—to their own destruction. (II Pet. 3:15b-16)

We see here that Paul's letters must be circulating in some collection. They are regarded as exhibiting enough holiness and wisdom to be included in a comparison with "the rest of scripture." Although there are themes in the letters common enough for the author of II Peter to expect his readers to recognize when he invokes them, there are enough difficulties or ambiguities to require careful and undistorted reading— that is, to require interpretation guided by other elements of the larger Christian story. No doubt the author of II Peter could confidently supply us with the correct interpretation! But the fact that Paul's letters from early on were seen to be both authoritative *and* in need of interpretation should be a healthy reminder of the never-ending task of recalling, interpreting, and retelling the Christian story in our own place and time.

When we attempt this task, living on the edge, we are drawn on and strengthened by the call to take it up and supported by our membership in a community of Christians whose stories stretch out in time and space beyond the local arenas of leadership. But in the collective experience of those who have led before us, we find more than encouragement along the way. We find dispositions for endurance and skills for the journey, strengths of character that might sustain women and men living on the edge, virtues whose practice might better equip us for the subversive vocation of a transforming ministry. And as we might suspect by now, we can get a glimpse of these virtues at work by turning once more to the letters of Paul.

Virtues for Life on the Edge

Paul's letter to Philemon is one of the more extraordinary documents in the Christian Scriptures precisely because of its perfectly ordinary character. Unlike Romans and Galatians, it expounds no heady doctrines. Unlike Philippians, it preserves no ancient liturgies. Unlike the Corinthian correspondence, it does not chronicle portentous conflicts crucial to the development of early Christianity. Instead, in its very ordinariness,

"Philemon opens a small but light-filled window on the Pauline mission."[2] It shows us far more than Paul's private appeal to a fellow Christian. It gives us a glimpse of Paul as a moral leader on the edge, exercising considerable skill and manifold virtues in the service of a transforming ministry. In fact, it shows us Paul's deep conviction that the story of Christ for which he is both prisoner and ambassador has the power to transform the world.[3]

Paul's short letter is loaded with persuasive conviction from its opening line. Paul, a "prisoner of Christ Jesus," writes with Timothy to "our dear fellow worker Philemon, our sister Apphia, our fellow soldier Archippus and the church that meets in your house" (Philem. 1-2). All these people, whose common bond is Christ, are drawn together in a shared identity in which each has a valuable place. Paul then gives thanks to God for Philemon "because I hear of the love and the faith which you have for the Lord Jesus and for all God's holy people" (Philem. 4-5), a faith and love that will be fully expressed in "all the good we can do for Christ" (Philem. 6). Philemon's share in the community of faith requires him to take an active role in doing good, and the fact that he has expressed his love in action enables Paul to say, "You have set the heart of God's holy people at rest" (Philem. 7).

Paul proceeds in the body of the letter to make a personal appeal to Philemon, and a very complex set of social and religious roles is involved in his request.[1] In his captivity Paul has met a man named Onesimus, who turns out to be Philemon's runaway slave. Onesimus has become a Christian and a valued fellow worker with Paul. Paul would like to keep Onesimus with him, out of the chains of slavery and in the chains of the gospel, but he acknowledges Philemon's rights in the matter and does not want to force what should be a spontaneous act of kindness (Philem. 14). Paul reminds Philemon that he could appeal to him on grounds of Christian duty (Philem. 8) or call him to account for the debt of new life in Christ that Philemon owes Paul (Philem. 19). "I am rather appealing to your love" for a "child of mine, whose father I became while wearing these chains" (Philem. 9-10). Onesimus, whose name in Greek means "useful," "was of no use to you before, but now he is useful both to you and to me" (Philem. 11). In Christ, Onesimus is at the same time Paul's child (Philem. 10) and a dear brother both to Paul and Philemon (Philem. 16). He is Paul's own heart, and Philemon's substitute in the service of the gospel (Philem. 12-13). Paul invites Philemon to acknowledge the transformation, not just in Onesimus's relation to Paul but to Philemon as well:

> I suppose you have been deprived of Onesimus for a time, merely so that you could have him back for ever, no longer as a slave, but something much better than a slave, a dear brother; especially dear to me, but how much more to you, both on the natural plane and in the Lord. So if you grant me any fellowship with yourself, welcome him as you would me. (Philem. 15-17)

Paul assures Philemon that if Onesimus owes Philemon anything—for his escape or for something he might have stolen—"I, Paul, shall pay it back" (Philem. 19). He tells his "brother" Philemon he is counting on him to "set my heart at rest, in Christ" (Philem. 20), echoing not only his identification of his own heart with Onesimus (Philem. 12) but also his opening address, where he praises Philemon for having "set the hearts of God's holy people at rest" (Philem. 7). Paul is offering Philemon a chance to continue acting in character, now toward Onesimus, and tells him, "I am writing with complete confidence in your compliance, sure that you will do even more than I ask" (Philem. 21).

In closing, Paul asks Philemon for a place to stay, saying, "I am hoping through your prayers to be restored to you" (Philem. 22). This personal request reminds Philemon that he may one day again greet Paul just as he is now being asked to greet Onesimus in Paul's place. Paul offers greetings from five fellow workers, thereby reminding Philemon of his place in the company of the saints, and ends by saying, "May the grace of our Lord Jesus Christ be with your spirit" (Philem. 25).

Paul, Onesimus, and Philemon are all living on the edge, and Philemon may come to realize that more clearly through Paul's letter and the challenge Onesimus now represents! Paul, once free, is now a slave for the gospel. Onesimus, once a slave, is now freed by the gospel and a brother to those in authority over him. Legally Onesimus is still a slave, subject to Philemon's will. Yet as he stands with his letter at the door to Philemon's house, it is Philemon who, facing him, stands at the more threatening threshold.

> The doorstep on which Philemon and Onesimus stand is the threshold of the church that meets in Philemon's house. If Philemon slams the door of his house in Onesimus' face in rejection of Paul's "appeal," he will be tacitly excluding himself from the house church into which he has retreated. . . . Standing there on his own doorstep, Philemon is a man on the threshold between two worlds.[5]

Philemon is suspended between the center of legal propriety and the edge of a radically new life in Christ, where the boundaries of law are blurred in the wild grace that makes all things new. If he greets Onesimus as a brother, he cannot treat him as a slave; if he treats him as a slave, he loses claim to membership in the church that meets in his own house. We do not have Philemon's reply to Paul. We do have Paul's prophetic vision of how Philemon was bound in Christ to reply to Onesimus, and it is a reply that would have fixed him firmly on the edge.

Like Philemon, surrounded by co-workers, receiving a letter from Paul, Christians today are not alone on the edge. Surrounded by the saints, we are also strengthened by virtues for life on the edge, virtues visible not only in Paul's letter to Philemon but also in the other stories of the saints we have been following as well. There we find offered to us the practice of humility, fidelity, practical wisdom, prophetic vision, hopeful solidarity, and love, living resources for life on the edge.[6]

It may seem strange to find humility in Paul, or Martin Luther King, Jr., or Alan Boesak, or a student pastor about to upset her church with aid to those with AIDS. But the humility we find in these stories is not the repugnant, groveling, self-abasing attitude whose modern attachment to the word "humility" has debased an ancient and powerful virtue.[7] The humility that empowers the minister as moral leader is a disposition formed in faith and guided by love that lets us see ourselves in a truthful relation to others, neither too high nor too low, by disciplining our vision with the insight that God loves *all* creation, sinners and saints and ordinary creatures alike. What God loves so deeply we humans can scarcely reject, and that, perhaps hardest of all, includes ourselves. Although we should not lord it over others, neither should we fail to assert our worth as God's beloved or fail to take up leadership when we are the vessels, however inadequate, from which the love of God may be poured out in the world.

Thus, Paul made bold in his humility to suggest that Philemon treat Onesimus no longer as a slave but as a brother. Martin Luther King made bold in his humility to suggest that the God who called Israel out of Egypt was the same God who calls blacks and whites out of their segregationist captivity in America. Alan Boesak makes bold in his humility to insist that the freedom of the Christian in God's love requires participation in the struggle for freedom of the neighbor we are called by God to love. The student pastor about to deliver her sermon on Jesus and the Syro-Phoenician woman makes bold in her humility to suggest that as Jesus learned from her, so we must learn today from people afflicted with AIDS but nonetheless loved by God.

In all of these stories, leadership on the edge grows out of humility, because the renunciation of status and the rejection of servile self-sacrifice enables the leader to see her or his position in the world with a truthful and radical clarity. If in humility Philemon sees truthfully the new spiritual relationships his embrace of the gospel brings with it, he can also see clearly the radical transformation in his social relations that gospel brings as well. And it is Paul's humility as one whose self-esteem was not dependent on his social roles but on his existence as a child of God that enabled him to see in Onesimus a fellow child and brother in Christ and in Philemon a fellow worker who now has the chance to embody Christian love in a radically transforming way. It is King's and Boesak's humility that leads them to uncover the lie that some people are inherently less valuable than others and so can be treated as means to the ends of their "superiors." And it is the student pastor's humility, experiencing herself and others as beloved children of God, that leads her to see discrimination toward persons with AIDS as an idolatrous preempting of God's judgment on God's creation.

The saints whose stories we have heard are also strengthened by the virtue of fidelity.[8] Paul continually called his readers back to the story of the good, asking them to hold on to what they had received but demanding also that they live toward the future in a faithful transformation of the present. He reminds Philemon of the acts of loving kindness that have given Philemon a good reputation among the faithful. Nonetheless, Paul's appeal shows that fidelity lies not in resting on the past but in faithfully carrying the story of the good into the future. Philemon will retain his place among those faithful to Christ not by adherence to a private, abstract belief but by his willingness to undertake concrete action in the world.

This is a strenuous fidelity, seeking to remain faithful even as it questions how the unfolding future speaks to the faith of the past. We remain faithful to the stories of the past not by repeating their conclusions but by carrying on the practice of Christian living today. Opponents of apartheid who condemn it as a heresy claim that those who practice it are not faithful to the living word of God. The minister watching the well-capping must choose between fidelity to the story of God's love for all and his local congregation's story of a highly selective love for some. The associate minister facing the divided social concerns committee also faces a lengthy and probably painful process of discernment, whose only alternative is an unfaithful silencing of the diverse voices in the community.[9]

As we saw in the last chapter, one person's fidelity may be another's betrayal. But in a world of constant uncertainty and change, we have no way of knowing once and for all the rightness of such claims. Practicing fidelity means exercising memory and imagination in the effort to hear other stories in conjunction with our own and thus to hear our own anew. Our continuing fidelity rests on our trust in God's promise to be with us always, and in our willingness always to test, as Paul was asking Philemon to do, whether the God of our Christian story *is* present in our lives. Nothing less will enable us to resist the idolatry that comes from presuming to know with certitude the mind of God.

In this discernment, the minister as moral leader needs to cultivate the virtue of practical wisdom.[10] The sermon that opens Martin Luther King, Jr.'s *Strength to Love* is titled "A Tough Mind and a Tender Heart."[11] He took for his text the admonition of Jesus, "Look, I am sending you out like sheep among wolves; so be cunning as snakes and yet innocent as doves" (Matt. 10:16). King knew this to be part of the instructions Jesus gives his disciples in sending them out on their mission of astonishing revelation. "Everything now covered up will be uncovered, and everything now hidden will be made clear. What I say to you in the dark, tell in the daylight; what you hear in whispers, proclaim from the housetops" (Matt. 10:26-27). King was aiming toward the transformation of his followers into moral leaders capable of shouting from the housetops of Birmingham and Washington, Atlanta and New York. He knew they must equip themselves for the task with a mind and heart both innocent and cunning. Their wisdom must be practical in this uncertain world, or it would not be wise at all.

As we have seen in the stories in this book, the practical wisdom that preserves moral leaders as sheep among the wolves is first and foremost a reflective skill, the practice of continually questioning whether the resources of the story of Christ are being brought to bear on the needs of the moment. "Whose story do I tell?" asks the preacher. "Whose truth do I teach?" asks the teacher. "Whose care do I seek?" asks the pastor. "Whose table do I set?" asks the priest. "Where does my allegiance lie?" asks the servant. Am I telling the story *in* the center or *from* the center? Am I open to new voices and new stories on the edge? Am I tempted not to lead or to betray the story of Christ that leads me on? And we have seen that humility and fidelity add their own practical questions, for they urge us to ask who we are in relation to others, and whether our community is moving faithfully forward in time toward the greater love of God and neighbor.

Paul's ability to speak so simply and powerfully to Philemon rested on his considerable practical wisdom in service to the gospel. As cunning as a snake, he makes subtle puns on Onesimus's name and puts Philemon in a position to see that if he rejected Paul's appeal, he rejected also the very church that met in his house. As innocent as a dove, he knew his appeal finally rested plainly on Philemon's share in the fellowship and love of God, and that no puns or manipulations could replace Philemon's own transformation in the light of that love. His innocent cunning was guided by his reflective awareness of what story, in fact, he told, and where in truth his allegiance lay, and of just how far out on the edge he was inviting Philemon to go in living out the love of God and neighbor.

Maintaining the balance of cunning and innocence is not easy. Practical wisdom in the Christian story needs always to be bounded and emboldened by the virtue of prophetic vision, the capacity to see things both as they are and as they might become in Christ. Such prophetic vision, as we have seen, is not the special gift of some, unavailable to others and therefore not required of them. It is rather a dimension of moral leadership inescapably part of the vocation of ministry in the first place, a call always to exercise imagination in the service of the gospel, never to be content with the consciousness offered by the status quo but always on the lookout for how things might look different from the new perspective of the edge.[12]

The minister answering his distraught parishioner on the telephone seems to fail at the exercise of prophetic vision. He hears her voice as a threat to the comfortable center he serves and is closed to the possibility that her suffering is part of his mission "to cure all kinds of disease and all kinds of illness" (Matt. 10:1). The minister watching the well-capping, in contrast, feels the stirring of prophetic vision in the realization that the story he sees being played out is not in faithful continuity with the story of Christ he is called to proclaim. The student pastor writing her sermon on Jesus and AIDS is exercising prophetic vision to extend what she knows about Jesus to a frightening and unexplored realm of the modern age. In the scenario of transforming leadership we explored in the story of the church with a legacy, both the pastor and the lay leaders of the church had to exercise prophetic vision to imagine themselves and their church moving into God's future. And certainly in the struggle for civil rights in America and against apartheid in South Africa, prophetic vision energizes and focuses the practical wisdom of the people of God, as they strive to transform the world that is toward the world it might become.

These last examples point to another virtue for life on the edge, a hopeful solidarity that is not ideological but rooted in a sense of radical community. The company of the saints that surrounds Paul at the beginning and end of the letter to Philemon surrounds Philemon as well and enables Paul to write with such gentle boldness and complete confidence. Hopeful solidarity is a way out of isolation, as well as a way into community. By hearing the stories of other restless hearts, we connect the past and present as we journey into the future and receive encouragement to go on. This hope for the beloved community is the reality that sustains Paul in shipwreck and captivity, Martin Luther King in prison and at his lonely midnight table, Alan Boesak in jail and under banning. His sense of membership in a wider Christian community helps the minister at the well muster the courage to call his local community into accountability to the local oppressed. The solidarity she feels for a church beyond single-issue politics gives hope to the associate minister facing the divided social concerns committee. A solidarity that exists firmly in hope has the power to call a present solidarity into existence for the student pastor confronted with the problem of AIDS. Certainly Linda, pursuing a lonely vocation among church structures where she stubbornly fails to fit, is given hope in this quest by her discovery of solidarity with a cloud of witnesses among the women who have faithfully embodied Christ for others in past and present.[13]

Such hopeful solidarity is a necessary virtue for life on the edge, exactly in that it connects us with others in a common bond far more vital to the future and frightening to the status quo than a sense of justice alone. Hopeful solidarity is impatient with the pace of justice, especially when the calculus of justice is hostage to the interests of the center. Justice may only ask how each may get his or her due, where hopeful solidarity insists that regardless of what is due me in a particular system of rights and privileges, my good is bound up with the good of others, and securing my just rights cannot be the end of my struggle.[14] Martin Luther King spoke much of justice, but it was the justice of the beloved community rather than of American democracy that he so fiercely desired, justice enfleshed with the body of Christ whose reality he could only grasp by hopeful solidarity with God and neighbor in a particular place and time.[15]

This is not to say that for Christians justice is not important. It is instead to claim that the story of Christ teaches us that justice, like freedom, is something we struggle for rather than something we begin with. We must be suspicious of disembodied claims of justice and of freedom, always asking whose justice is served, whose freedom is defended. It should be a warning, for example, that the Ministry of Justice enforces apartheid in South Africa.[16] The virtue of hopeful solidarity not only sustains us in times of loneliness and isolation but also offers us a concrete sense of what the beloved community is like, so that we may not be seduced by the claims of the center that heaven has arrived on earth.

"I am rather appealing to your love" (Philem. 9). Hopeful solidarity with Christians before us and all God's creatures surrounding us reminds us we are still restless hearts on a journey toward love. Paul makes his appeal to Philemon in love and to love. He reminds us that the most fundamental of the virtues for the minister as moral leader—and for all who seek the God revealed in Christ—is at the same time our destination, our way there, and our bread and wine for the journey. Our experience of God's love, announced in the story of Christ and given shape in the stories of others who seek to love as God loves, enables us to practice humility, gives meaning to our fidelity, shapes our exercise of practical wisdom, sharpens our prophetic vision, and gives substance to our hopeful solidarity. Drawing us out of ourselves, the love of God and neighbor becomes the story of our hearts, and therein lies the heart of the story I am telling here.

Story of the Heart, Heart of the Story

Throughout this book I have been using the image of a journey to depict the setting of moral leadership, a journey that pulls us along edge and center of the communities with which we travel. Whether we feel ourselves to be wandering aimlessly in some dark wood or sitting securely near a warm fire, our lives are constituted by constant change. Homeless wandering exacts a more tangible toll, but in trying to sustain the comfort of the hearth, we find we can't burn the same log twice. Our hearts become restless. Worn out in striving, we are unable to secure ourselves against the accidents of history and the relentless onrush of time. We find ourselves impelled on some sort of movement, some kind of journey, even when we would rather devote ourselves to sitting still.

The journey we undertake may not take us into new lands, though like the Exodus of old and the civil rights marches of this century, it may move us across boundary lines as distinct as the Red Sea or the bridge at Selma. Nonetheless, even journeys that lap up physical distance are fundamentally journeys of the heart. Our restless hearts long for direction and purpose in a world tragically lacking in each. They find that direction in the great stories of the good that offer a vision of life as it might be if only we shape ourselves to become the kind of people capable of living it well.

But as we have seen repeatedly, such stories of the good are told in human communities over time and are themselves subject to the forces of fragmentation and change that make our hearts restless in the first place. There is no one story of the good that without question stands over and unifies all others, even though many communities have tried to make that claim in an effort to secure a center against time and change. There are instead a multitude of stories that compete for the allegiance of our hearts, offering purpose and destination to our movement, calling us to become different kinds of people, and to live out, rather than merely to assert, the truth of the stories as a truth about the possibilities of human existence.

Each of these great stories is told in many voices, which both compel and confuse our restless hearts. Within the framework of the Christian story, we are confronted at the outset with dozens of books bearing the witness of the Hebrew people, four canonical Gospels telling the most basic Christian narrative in distinct voices, letters collected from the earliest

Christian communities giving us a glimpse into complicated worlds, and with hundreds of years of hearing, telling, and retelling the story of Christ through the often discordant voices of an unruly cloud of witnesses.

In looking at the Christian minister as a moral leader, we have been seeing her or him as one who listens to the aspirations of restless hearts and to the stories that offer them purpose and direction. We have been overhearing leaders who interpret the history of a people in the strong light of a story of the love of God and neighbor toward which those people might move. And finally, we have been listening to leaders who struggle to retell the story of Christ in a clear and compelling way, without narrowing down or betraying its richness and complexity by refusing to listen to the many voices in which the story is told.

Along the way we have heard the stories of ministers struggling to live out their calling to a vocation of leadership, and of communities trying to become the kind of people capable of loving God and neighbor. We have met a minister caught between defending the center of his community and responding to a painful phone call from a woman dangerously on the edge of it. We have seen a minister watching a well-capping, wondering how to respond to an event that runs counter to the stories that have nurtured him in Christ. We have seen a student pastor suspended in a network of expectations that would have her fail some in meeting others and have seen her senior pastor fearing the conflict and change that open assistance to people with AIDS would surely bring. We have seen an associate minister facing a split within her church brought on by two distinct readings of the Christian story, each of which would have her church be a different kind of community. We have met Linda, who heard her call in community yet finds it hard to live her vocation in institutions more attuned to defending the center than responding to the edge. We have reflected on the risky opportunities an unexpected legacy posed for an urban congregation and saw risks that had to be shared by leaders and followers alike if the journey of the congregation as a Christian community was to be held on course. We have seen two other communities discovering their character, and the character of the institutional church of which they are a part, in the process of choosing new leaders.

We have seen that people responding to the call to ministry can receive powerful support through critical reflection on inherited images of the minister, and through the questions those images raise about the role of the minister as moral leader in the formation of the beloved community. We have seen that moral leadership strives to tell the story in the center of the community and thereby preserve and maintain the quality of life within the accepted vision of the community. Yet we have also seen that the vocation of leadership in ministry must go beyond transaction to transformation, as it seeks to turn leaders and followers alike into a people ever more reponsive to God's love.

We have encountered "our dear brother Paul" and seen in his wrestling with the leadership of some of the earliest Christian communities problems and possibilities that exist today in our own, as we try to tell the story of the good in the center and on the edge of our diverse communities. We have had glimpses of leaders like Martin Luther King, Jr., and Alan Boesak, as they try to tell the story of Christ anew in their place and time, resisting the temptation not to lead and the temptation to betray. We have seen others who failed to resist these temptations, falling prey to the deceptive comfort of the center or so far resisting the wild grace of the God who calls us to love the neighbor as to enslave and kill the neighbor in God's name. We have discerned in these stories of the saints virtues for living a life on the edge today.

All these people have been trying to live out a journey begun when a story of the good beckoned their restless hearts. The journey of the heart seldom has a fixed beginning. We may or may not be able to recall when each of us consciously began to participate in the quest, but stories of the good have been told to us from childhood. We learn them and are shaped by them long before we can take part in their telling. As tangled as these stories can become in our own lives, it is even harder for us to tell when the great stories themselves began. Humankind has been surrounded and sustained by stories of the good from as far back as memory allows us to go, farther back even than the eye of the archaeologist can trace on the walls of caves and the placing of bones in the grave. What we loosely call "the Christian story" itself does not begin with Christ but is part of the continuing story of a people called by God on a journey long ago.

As it is with beginnings, so it is with endings. The destination of the heart is not a place that can be reached and rested in, a center finally found that can thereafter be secured. Our restless hearts seek a purpose, not a place. Their longed-for destination is not a point to arrive at but a direction to the journey through time that will not cease until time releases its hold on us. Even when we slip into death, many of the great stories, the Christian story among them, tell us the end of the story has not yet been reached. And even when *we* die, the journey of our fellow human beings continues, and the story that can be told of us becomes part of the questing of those who continue on the never-ending journey.

All of this means that when we begin to take conscious part in our journeying, it is like waking up and finding ourselves already walking on some barely discernible path. We have a lot of catching up to do, finding out what stories have laid claim to our hearts, how each would have us live, and what direction to follow now that we are awake. The minister as moral leader helps the community she or he would lead to engage in this difficult process of discernment, deliberation, and direction. The minister who lives at the center of the community will scarcely be aware of the possibilities of movement at the edge. She will not be able to assist in the community's deliberation, because she will not hear the other voices in which the story of the good is told, let alone be open to the voices of other stories. He will not be able to find a direction in which to keep moving, for he will become too bound to the defense of the place he has arrived at, a place that time and change will surely slip away from under his feet.

The hardships that Paul described in the life of an apostle may well become the lot of the minister as moral leader today. We can take strength from his example and bear the problems of life on the edge not for our own sake but for the sake of the story that called us out from the illusory safety of the center in the first place. We hope that in living on the edge, we might tell the story of our hearts all the more truthfully and in doing so help lead others to the heart of the story that calls us all.

Living on the edge means taking up as a way of life the insistent questing that most of us dread to face at all. Yet the disposition to carry on this quest, this movement out from our centers and forward into the edges of time, is nothing less than unsentimentalized love for God and neighbor. Loving God and neighbor means nothing if we do not seek to bear the image of God and to serve the needs of the neighbor. Love is the most vulnerable of all feelings because of its absolute dependence on something outside ourselves over which, in loving, we must renounce control. But love becomes the most powerful of the virtues when its object is the God revealed in Christ, a God who beckons us in the stories of the saints to take up an endless journey and along the way to become a people capable of loving well. The best resource for the journey lies in keeping our true destination, the love of God and neighbor, firmly fixed in our hearts, so that, as our dear brother Paul reminds us, our "fellowship in faith may come to expression in full knowledge of all the good we can do for Christ" (Philem. 6).

The minister as moral leader makes bold to shout from the housetops the good news of the gospel, and to lead the restless hearts who respond to the story of the love of God revealed in Christ. We attempt this in our uncertain world with the encouragement and the confidence passed on by the stories of the saints. Our restless hearts take heart in the knowledge that all God's holy people send their greetings to us along the way. With the love of God and neighbor our destination and our way, we can move on, firmly held in the grace of the Lord Jesus Christ, the love of God, and the fellowship of the Holy Spirit that is with us all, even to the end of time.

NOTES

1. Restless Hearts: The Challenge of Moral Leadership

1. The complexity of stories thus at the same time requires and facilitates the exercise of critical reflection. For a variety of perspectives on the function of stories, see W. J. T. Mitchell, ed., *On Narrative* (Chicago: University of Chicago Press, 1981); George Stroup, *The Promise of Narrative Theology* (Atlanta: John Knox Press, 1981); Michael Goldberg, *Theology and Narrative* (Nashville: Abingdon Press, 1982); William Bausch, *Storytelling, Imagination, and Faith* (Mystic, Conn.: Twenty-Third Century Publications, 1984); and Paul Nelson, *Narrative and Morality* (University Park: Penn State Press, 1987). See also the works cited in notes 3 and 4 below.

2. Herbert Gutman, *The Black Family in Slavery and Freedom* (New York: Pantheon Books, 1976); Rosemary Radford Ruether and Eleanor McLaughlin, eds., *Women of Spirit: Female Leadership in the Jewish and Christian Traditions* (New York: Simon & Schuster, 1979); Dante Alighieri, *The Divine Comedy*, trans. and ed. by Thomas G. Bergin (New York: Appleton-Century-Crofts, 1955); Umberto Eco, *The Name of the Rose* (New York: Harcourt Brace Jovanovich, 1983); Marion Zimmer Bradley, *The Mists of Avalon* (New York: Ballantine Books, 1982); Graham Greene, *Monsignor Quixote* (New York: Washington Square Press, 1983).

3. For a sampling of such grand and compelling stories, see Robert S. Ellwood, Jr., ed., *Words of the World's Religions* (Englewood Cliffs, N.J.: Prentice-Hall, 1977). On interpreting stories and the human cultures they represent and shape, see Clifford Geertz, *The Interpretation of Cultures* (New York: Basic Books, 1973), and Victor Turner, *The Ritual Process* (Ithaca, N.Y.: Cornell University Press, 1969). The interplay of character, virtue, and stories has been a major theme in the work of Stanley Hauerwas, especially in *Vision and Virtue* (Notre Dame: Fides Publishers, 1974); *Character and the Christian Life*, 2nd ed. (San Antonio, Tex.: Trinity University Press, 1985); *Truthfulness and Tragedy*, with Richard Bondi and David Burrell (Notre Dame: University of Notre Dame Press, 1977); *Community of Character* (Notre Dame: University of Notre Dame Press, 1981);

Peaceable Kingdom (Notre Dame: University of Notre Dame Press, 1983); and *Christian Existence Today* (Durham, N.C.: Labyrinth Press, 1988).

4. On the way stories form the heart, see Richard Bondi, "The Elements of Character," *Journal of Religious Ethics* 12, no. 4 (1984): 201-18. On the many voices of the Christian story, see Garrett Green, ed., *Scriptural Authority and Narrative Interpretation* (Philadelphia: Fortress Press, 1987). Good examples of the use of stories in doing theological ethics are found in Karen Lebacqz, *Professional Ethics: Power and Paradox* (Nashville: Abingdon Press, 1985), and James Wm. McClendon, Jr., *Systematic Theology: Ethics* (Nashville: Abingdon Press, 1986). An especially good account of the interaction of literary criticism, anthropology, and biblical studies, important to my use of Scripture in this book, is found in the introduction to Norman Petersen, *Rediscovering Paul: Philemon and the Sociology of Paul's Narrative World* (Philadelphia: Fortress Press, 1985), pp. 1-42. On the role of the theologian as interpreter of stories, see Luke Johnson, *Decision Making in the Church: A Biblical Model* (Philadelphia: Fortress Press, 1983).

5. On the situation in Corinth, see Gerd Theissen, *The Social Setting of Pauline Christianity* (Philadelphia: Fortress Press, 1982). The "Letter from Birmingham City Jail" is found in *A Testament of Hope: The Essential Writings of Martin Luther King, Jr.*, ed. by James M. Washington (New York: Harper & Row, 1986), pp. 289-302. Several of Alan Boesak's most important writings against apartheid are collected in *Black and Reformed: Apartheid, Liberation, and the Calvinist Tradition* (Maryknoll, N.Y.: Orbis Books, 1984).

6. This is one of the themes in Walter Brueggemann's richly provocative book, *The Prophetic Imagination* (Philadelphia: Fortress Press, 1978). He sees the prophets of the Hebrew and Christian Scriptures as agents for the transformation of consciousness, awakening people from the illusory security of a "royal consciousness" and energizing them for the formation of alternative communities where the stories of God may be truthfully told and lived out.

7. Blaming the victim is a particular problem in the way individuals and communities respond to sexual and domestic violence, as they attempt to silence the victims whose broken bones and spirits give the lie to the story of the good, or at least to its embodiment in the blaming community. On this see Marie Fortune, *Sexual Violence: The Unmentionable Sin* (New York: Pilgrim Press, 1984).

8. That God as the center of all value relativizes all human centers has been emphasized by H. Richard Niebuhr, especially in the essays collected in *Radical Monotheism and Western Culture* (New York: Harper & Row, 1970). For detailed treatments of the idolatry of holding to human centers, see Stanley Hauerwas, *Against the Nations* (New York: Crossroads, 1985); John Howard Yoder, *The Priestly Kingdom* (Notre Dame: University of Notre Dame Press, 1984); Rosemary Radford Ruether, *Sexism and God-Talk* (Boston: Beacon Press, 1983); and Walter Brueggemann, *Israel's Praise* (Philadelphia: Fortress Press, 1987).

9. On the story of the good Samaritan, see Joseph A. Fitzmeyer, *The Gospel According to Luke X–XXIV*, Anchor Bible no. 28A (New York: Doubleday, 1985), pp. 882-90. Fitzmeyer notes that Jesus turns the thrust of the lawyer's question away from "Who is *my* neighbor?" toward "How am *I* to be a neighbor to others?"

10. Three important sources converge here, all of which will be explored in the pages to follow. Seeing life as an ongoing quest for a resting place of the heart was an organizing motif for Augustine's *Confessions*, trans. by R. S. Pine-Coffin (Baltimore: Penguin Books, 1973). Trying to tell a truthful story out of the interweaving of our corporate history with the story of God in Christ was a concern of H. Richard Niebuhr in such works as *The Meaning of Revelation* (New York: Macmillan, 1941), *Christ and Culture* (New York: Harper & Row, 1951), *The Purpose of the Church and Its Ministry* (New York: Harper & Row, 1956), *Radical Monotheism,* and *The Responsible Self* (New York: Harper & Row, 1963). Viewing leadership as the purposeful shaping of social change over time, in the direction of shared goals grounded in the needs, wants, and deep aspirations of leaders and followers, is a primary theme in James MacGregor Burns, *Leadership* (New York: Harper & Row, 1978).

11. On conflict as a catalyst for change in consciousness and the resulting possibilities for moral leadership, see Burns, *Leadership*, pp. 1-48.

12. On the transformation of moral possibilities through a shift in consciousness of experience, see the essays collected in B. Andolsen, C. Gudorf, and M. Pellauer, ed., *Women's Consciousness, Women's Conscience* (New York: Winston Press, 1985).

13. Augustine, *Confessions*, Book 1, chapter 1, p. 21. For further exploration of the restless yearning of Augustine's heart and how that became a primary metaphor for his theology, see Peter Brown, *Augustine of Hippo* (Berkeley: University of California Press, 1967), esp. pp. 158-83.

14. On the distinctiveness of the Lucan account of the Great Commandment, see Fitzmeyer, *Gospel According to Luke X–XXIV*, pp.

876-82. "Jesus' confirmation of the lawyer's double response makes the double commandment of love into a norm for the conduct of the Christian disciple" (p. 878).

15. H. R. Niebuhr, *The Purpose of the Church and Its Ministry*, p. 39.

2. Hearing the Call

1. For a general interpretation of the placement of these stories in early Christian literature, see Luke T. Johnson, *The Writings of the New Testament* (Philadelphia: Fortress Press, 1985), pp. 197-240 (Luke-Acts) and pp. 302-14 (Galatians); for detailed commentary on the stories in Acts, see Ernst Haenchen, *The Acts of the Apostles* (Philadelphia: Westminster Press, 1971), pp. 318-29 (Acts 9:1-19a), pp. 623-31 (Acts 22:1-16), and pp. 680-94 (Acts 26:9-18); on Galatians, see Hans Dieter Betz, *Galatians* (Philadelphia: Fortress Press, 1979), pp. 57-84 (Gal. 1:12-24).

2. For a classical understanding of vocation as a personal call in a corporate context, see Thomas Oden, *Pastoral Theology* (New York: Harper & Row, 1983), pp. 18-46. On vocation as purposeful life-work and on the universality of "call" and the particularity of "vocation," see Lynn N. Rhodes, *Co-Creating* (Philadelphia: Westminster Press, 1987), pp. 100-121.

3. On the formative role of vocation in the life of an individual and its relation to the larger Christian story, see James W. Fowler, *Becoming Adult, Becoming Christian* (New York: Harper & Row, 1984). On the role of stories in forming character and on the normative force of what stories are kept alive in shaping our understanding of the nature of the church and the tasks of its ministers, see Hauerwas, *Community of Character* and *Christian Existence Today*.

4. The importance of critical reflection on the stories of women ministers for transforming our understanding of the vocation of ministry is emphasized by Rhodes, *Co-Creating*, and in the essays collected in Judith Weidman, *Women Ministers* (New York: Harper & Row, 1985). Recovering those stories from a tradition that has suppressed them is undertaken in Ruether and McLaughlin, *Women of Spirit*, and weaving newly heard stories into new ministerial practices is an important concern in Rosemary Radford Ruether, *Women-Church* (New York: Harper & Row, 1985).

5. On traditional images of the minister and related offices of ministry, see Oden, *Pastoral Theology*, pp. 49-84. For a broad historical account of important images and offices, see H. Richard Niebuhr, Daniel D. Williams, and Sydney E. Ahlstrom, *The Ministry in Historical Perspectives* (New York: Harper & Row, 1983). The orchestration of roles and expectations in ministry as a profession is given detailed treatment in Lebacqz, *Professional Ethics*.

6. "Pastoral Director" was proposed by Niebuhr, *The Purpose of the*

Church and Its Ministry. "Shepherd" is an organizing image for Oden, *Pastoral Theology.* "Pastoral Interpreter" is an image drawn from Charles Gerkin, *Widening the Horizons* (Philadelphia: Westminster Press, 1986). "Practical Theologian" is the suggestion of Joseph C. Hough, Jr., and John B. Cobb, Jr., *Christian Identity and Theological Education* (Chico, Ca.: Scholars Press, 1985). "Partners in the Household of Freedom" is drawn from Letty Russell, *Household of Freedom* (Philadelphia: Westminster Press, 1987). "Co-Creators in the New Creation" is taken from Rhodes, *Co-Creating.* The five classical images I am about to explore are often grouped with a sixth, "Prophet." For reasons to be developed in subsequent chapters, I am not isolating "prophet" as a separate image, because I will argue there ought to be a prophetic dimension to the exercise of *all* the images of a minister. Separating it out gives the impression that being prophetic is "someone else's job" to those whose primary identity is preacher, teacher, and so on.

7. Two important statements of the task and practice of preaching are found in Fred Craddock, *Preaching* (Nashville: Abingdon Press, 1985), and David Buttrick, *Homiletic* (Philadelphia: Fortress Press, 1987). A good example of the essential role of narrative in preaching the Christian story is found in Gail R. O'Day, *The Word Disclosed: John's Story and Narrative Preaching* (St. Louis: CBP Press, 1987).

8. The work of Thomas Groome, *Christian Religious Education: Sharing Our Story and Vision* (New York: Harper & Row, 1980), has been especially influential in seeing the minister as teacher in transmitting the Christian story. See also Craig Dykstra, *Vision and Character* (New York: Paulist Press, 1981).

9. Such dispute over the correct interpretation of the inherited wisdom of the past, focused on New Testament and patristic sources, functions to mount a critique of present-day church teaching in Edward Schillebeeckx, *The Church with a Human Face* (New York: Crossroad, 1985). For a similar reinterpretation of traditional images and offices drawn from taking seriously the teaching found in hearing previously ignored voices of women, see Ruether and McLaughlin, *Women of Spirit,* and Ruether, *Women-Church.*

10. Such reliance on discernment for guidance in the Christian community's reading of biblical texts is discussed in detail in Johnson, *Decision Making in the Church,* and forms a significant part of Schillebeeckx's argument in *The Church with a Human Face.*

11. On the role of the pastor in governance and counsel, see Oden, *Pastoral Theology,* pp. 169-223. Other helpful statements emphasizing pastoral care include John Patton, *Pastoral Counseling: A Ministry of the Church* (Nashville: Abingdon Press, 1983), and Gerkin, *Widening the Horizons;* emphasizing pastoral governance are Thomas C. Campbell and Gary B. Reierson, *The Gift of Administration* (Philadelphia:

Westminster Press, 1981), and James D. Anderson and Ezra Earl Jones, *The Management of Ministry* (New York: Harper & Row, 1978).

12. See, for example, Ruether, *Sexism and God-Talk,* Rhodes, *Co-Creating,* and Russell, *Household of Freedom.*

13. For an historical account of the image of "priest" that is sensitive to hierarchical distortion of the image, see Schillebeeckx, *The Church with a Human Face.*

14. For contemporary ecumenical appropriation of the image of priest, see Earl E. Shelp and Ronald H. Sunderland, *The Pastor as Priest* (New York: Pilgrim Press, 1987).

15. An influential treatment of the servant image, drawn from an attempt to transform the manager-employee relation, is Robert K. Greenleaf, *Servant Leadership* (New York: Paulist Press, 1977).

16. On discriminating "servant" from other images of the minister, see Oden, *Pastoral Theology.* Reflection on the biblical roots of the servant image and its contemporary appropriation is found in Earl E. Shelp and Ronald H. Sunderland, *The Pastor as Servant* (New York: Pilgrim Press, 1986). The relative powerlessness of the minister as servant, in the sense of rejecting status and the power of impersonal authority, is held in tension in the modern world with the structural power often given to (or taken by) "professionals." This tension has been well explored by Lebacqz, *Professional Ethics,* pp. 109-51.

3. Transforming Ministry

1. See the discussion of this passage by Elizabeth Schussler Fiorenza, "Word, Spirit, and Power," in Ruether and McLaughlin, *Women of Spirit,* pp. 29-70.

2. On dating the Thessalonian correspondence, see Johnson, *The Writings of the New Testament,* pp. 260-72, and Pheme Perkins, "1 Thessalonians" and "2 Thessalonians," in James L. Mays, ed., *Harper's Bible Commentary* (New York: Harper & Row, 1988), pp. 1230-36.

3. On this point see Theissen, "Legitimation and Subsistence: An Essay on the Sociology of Early Christian Missionaries," in *The Social Setting of Pauline Christianity,* pp. 27-67.

4. Here I have been exploring aspects of the growing "professionalism" of contemporary ministry, which gains social respectability and status at the cost of adopting dominant social attitudes toward the nature of "professional services" today. Related problems are explored in Dennis Campbell, *Doctors, Lawyers, Ministers: Christian Ethics in Professional Practice* (Nashville: Abingdon Press, 1982); Lebacqz, *Professional Ethics;* Hough and Cobb, *Christian Identity and Theological Education;* and Gaylord Noyce, *Pastoral Ethics: Professional Responsibilities of the Clergy* (Nashville: Abingdon Press, 1988).

5. On the way different stories contend for the formation of character in the same community, see Hauerwas, *Community of*

Character. On finding the story of a particular community, see the case study and critical commentaries in Carl S. Dudley, ed., *Building Effective Ministry: Theory and Practice in the Local Church* (New York: Harper & Row, 1983). On assessing the impact of the dominant story in shaping the self-identity and mission of a local congregation, see David A. Roozen, William McKinney, and Jackson W. Carroll, *Varieties of Religious Presence* (New York: Pilgrim Press, 1984). And on using the language of larger, "mythic" stories in trying to shape character in community, see James F. Hopewell, *Congregation: Stories and Structures* (Philadelphia: Fortress Press, 1987).

6. Burns notes that transactional leadership "occurs when one person takes the initiative in making contact with others for the purpose of an exchange of valued things" (*Leadership,* p. 19). In the present case, the valued things were initially the three plans for the use of the bequest. The pastor was able to add a fourth valued thing, a sense of continuity with the story of the congregation, and use that to broker the exchange of the other three desires. For a detailed analysis of transactional leadership, see Burns, pp. 257-397.

7. Power-wielding is thus a distortion of leadership because it divorces the aims and interests of followers from leaders, or only takes followers' concerns into account as it benefits the power-wielder's separate aims. Power-wielding also divorces power itself, or the ability to get things done, from the longer-term moral purpose that helps communities decide *what* things ought to be done and *why.* On power-wielding, see Burns, *Leadership,* pp. 1-48.

8. Burns describes transforming leadership as follows: "Leaders can also shape and alter and elevate the motives and values and goals of followers through the vital *teaching* role of leadership. This is *transforming* leadership. The premise of this leadership is that, whatever the separate interests persons might hold, they are presently or potentially united in the pursuit of "higher" goals, the realization of which is tested by the achievement of significant change that represents the collective or pooled interests of leaders and followers" (*Leadership,* pp. 425-26; emphasis in original). For a detailed analysis of transforming leadership, see Burns, pp. 141-256, 401-64.

9. Martin Luther King, Jr., *Strength to Love* (Philadelphia: Fortress Press, 1982), pp. 23-24.

4. The Minister as Moral Leader

1. Stanislaw Lem, *The Cyberiad: Fables for a Cybernetic Age* (New York: Avon, 1976), p. 170.

2. On the meaning and function of parables, see John R. Donahue, *The Gospel in Parable* (Philadelphia: Fortress Press, 1988), pp. 1-27. The account of Augustine's conversion is found in Book 8 of *The Confessions,* pp. 157-79. On hearing another conversion story,

Augustine notes, "When your servant Simplicianus told me the story of Victorinus, I began to glow with fervor to imitate him. This, of course, was why Simplicianus had told it to me" (p. 164). See also Brown, *Augustine of Hippo*, pp. 158-83. On Antony and other stories from early monasticism, see Roberta C. Bondi, *To Love as God Loves* (Philadelphia: Fortress Press, 1987). Finally, for an analysis of the parable of the good Samaritan, with a concern for its contemporary appropriation, see Donahue, *The Gospel in Parable*, pp. 128-34.

3. King, *Strength to Love*, p. 113.

4. King originally told the story in *Stride Toward Freedom* (New York: Harper & Row, 1987) before working it into the sermons collected in *Strength to Love*. David Garrow, though perhaps too quick to stress this incident over other moments of revelation in King's life, treats King's midnight experience in his *Bearing the Cross* (New York: William Morrow, 1986), pp. 56-58, 75. On other biblical images and metaphors that helped form King's character, see James McClendon, *Biography as Theology* (Nashville: Abingdon Press, 1974).

5. See also Yahweh's assurances to Abram, Genesis 15:1; Isaac, Genesis 26:24; Jacob, Genesis 46:1-4; and Moses, Exodus 3:11-12. I was helped in seeing King's reliance on this assurance in his preaching by Gail R. O'Day, "'Do Not Be Afraid': Preaching as Salvation Oracle" (unpublished manuscript).

6. King, *Strength to Love*, p. 112. On storytelling and preaching, see Fred Craddock, *Preaching*, and Edward A. Steimle, Morris J. Niedenthal, and Charles Rice, *Preaching the Story* (Philadelphia: Fortress, 1980).

7. On the collection in Antioch reported in Acts, see Haenchen, *Acts*, pp. 373-79. On the collection in the Corinthian correspondence, see Victor Paul Furnish, *II Corinthians*, Anchor Bible No. 32A (New York: Doubleday, 1984), pp. 384-455.

8. The reconstruction of the Corinthian correspondence I have followed in this book is that of Furnish, *II Corinthians*, pp. 4-57.

9. Thus, telling the story in the center is basically a form of transactional leadership, though its appeal to the implicit demands of a common story shows it moving on the way to transforming leadership. For a good example of telling the story in the center with what I will call later a prophetic angle of vision, see Dieter Hessel, *Social Ministry* (Philadelphia: Westminster Press, 1982).

10. On the temptation to reduce moral leadership to a series of transactions ground out by a bureaucracy, see Burns, *Leadership*, pp. 287-307.

11. These and other temptations to abandon moral leadership will be treated at greater length in chapter 5.

12. King, "Letter from Birmingham City Jail," in *A Testament of Hope*, pp. 289-302. Quotations in the following paragraphs are from these pages.

13. Ibid., p. 302.

14. See Brueggemann, *Prophetic Imagination*; Schussler Fiorenza, "Word, Spirit, and Power;" George W. MacRae, "Paul, Prophet and Spiritual Leader," in *Pastor as Prophet*, pp. 99-113, along with other essays in that book; and Carl S. Dudley and Earle Hilgert, "The Energy of Countercultural Christianity," in *New Testament Tensions and the Contemporary Church* (Philadelphia: Fortress Press, 1987), pp. 38-75.

15. Brueggemann, *Prophetic Imagination*, pp. 13, 12.

16. Ibid., p. 13.

17. For King's own reflection on what led him to this path, see, among many valuable documents collected in *A Testament of Hope*, "Pilgrimage to Nonviolence", pp. 35-40, and King's 1965 *Playboy* interview, pp. 340-77.

18. Indeed, this is the sort of situation out of which liberation theology and feminist theology might be born. On liberation theology, see Rebecca Chopp, *The Praxis of Suffering* (Maryknoll, N.Y.: Orbis Books, 1986). On feminist theology, see the authors cited in note 22 below.

19. Quoted by Washington in *A Testament of Hope*, p. 217.

20. King, "I Have a Dream," *A Testament of Hope*, pp. 217-220.

21. See, for example, King's comments on nuclear disarmament in "The Answer to a Perplexing Question," *Strength to Love*, pp. 127-37, and his explicit stance against American policy in Vietnam, "A Time to Break Silence," *A Testament of Hope*, pp. 231-244.

22. The voices Linda hears are as follows: In biblical studies, Elizabeth Schussler-Fiorenza, *In Memory of Her* (New York: Crossroad, 1984). In historical studies, Rosemary Radford Ruether, ed., *Religion and Sexism* (New York: Simon & Schuster, 1974). Important writings of Julian include *Julian of Norwich: Showings*, trans. Edmund Colledge and James Walsh (New York: Paulist Press, 1978), with a contemporary appropriation in Julia Gatta, *Three Spiritual Directors* (Cambridge, Mass.: Cowley Pub., 1986). In theological studies, Rosemary Radford Ruether, *Sexism and God Talk* (Boston: Beacon Press, 1983), and Sallie McFague, *Models of God* (Philadelphia: Fortress Press, 1987). In psychology and pastoral care, Carol Gilligan, *In a Different Voice* (Cambridge, Mass.: Harvard University Press, 1982), and Mary D. Pellauer, Barbara Chester, and Jane Boyajian, *Sexual Assault and Abuse: A Handbook for Clergy and Professionals* (New York: Harper & Row, 1987). In theological ethics, Andolsen et al., *Women's Consciousness, Women's Conscience*; Lebacqz, *Professional Ethics*; and Margaret A. Farley, *Personal Commitments* (New York: Harper & Row, 1986). And in pastoral theology and worship, Rhodes, *Co-Creating*, and Ruether, *Women-Church*.

23. Linda's friend might suggest she read Earl Shelp, Ronald Sunderland, and Peter Mansell, *AIDS: Personal Stories in Pastoral Perspective* (New York: Pilgrim Press, 1986), and Earl Shelp and

Ronald Sunderland, *AIDS and the Church* (Philadelphia: Westminster Press, 1987).

24. Linda could find such information about Mark and the story of the Syro-Phoenician woman in Johnson, *The Writings of the New Testament*, pp. 147-71, and in John R. Donahue, "Mark," *Harper's Bible Commentary*, pp. 983-1009. It is hearing Mark in conjunction with the voice of her friend that transforms the text and, in doing so, transforms her.

25. Thus, at issue here is not just the formation of the canon but the use of the "Bible" as a text for the church. Luke Johnson has written helpfully on these themes in *Decision Making in the Church* and in "The New Testament as the Church's Book," *The Writings of the New Testament*, pp. 530-52.

5. The Temptation Not to Lead

1. Having looked in chapter 4 at Paul's handling of the collection, I now look at his relationship to the community as a whole. A third aspect of the Corinthian situation, Paul's trouble with the "super-apostles," will be taken up in chapter 6. As noted earlier, I am following Furnish, *II Corinthians*, in my understanding of the order of events in Corinth.

2. For an assessment of Paul's leadership in Corinth, see Doohan, *Leadership in Paul,* pp. 111-18.

3. For a discussion of the accidents of history and their role in the formation of character in individuals and communities, see Richard Bondi, "The Elements of Character."

4. On locating the story of a congregation, see Hopewell, *Congregation*, Dudley, *Building Effective Ministry*, and Jackson Carroll, et al., *Handbook for Congregational Analysis* (Nashville: Abingdon Press, 1986).

5. The discovery of the story that has been truly shaping one's character and the process of action followed by reflection that leads to the discovery is given tragic expression in John LeCarre, *A Perfect Spy* (New York: Alfred A. Knopf, 1986), where truth comes too late for redemption. The possibility that our stories may become redemptive to other people by giving them critical insight into their own is given a melancholy yet hopeful treatment in Greene, *Monsignor Quixote.*

6. Thus Hauerwas's emphasis on the need to form communities where people can tell the truth to one another about themselves and the world; see, for example, *Truthfulness and Tragedy* and *Christian Existence Today.*

7. An attempt to formulate biblically based structures of leadership that, in my terms, enables the Christian story to be told by the *community* without paralyzing individual leaders is found in John Howard Yoder, "The Hermeneutics of Peoplehood: A Protestant

Perspective," in *The Priestly Kingdom* (Notre Dame: University of Notre Dame Press, 1984), pp. 15-45.

8. The conflicts that arise between the corporate identity of a church and its mission as a Christian community are discussed by Melvin Williams, "The Conflict of Corporate Church and Spiritual Community," in Dudley, *Building Effective Ministry,* pp. 55-67. On discerning whether the life of a church reflects its Christian identity amid social pressures toward conformity, see Hessel, *Social Ministry,* pp. 13-76.

9. The text of the sermon is found in Ronald J. Sider and Darrel J. Brubaker, *Preaching on Peace* (Philadelphia: Fortress Press, 1982), pp. 29-33. Quotations in the following paragraphs are all from these pages.

10. See King's sermon "Our God is Able" in *Strength to Love,* pp. 106-14. On the necessity of pride and its relation to the story of a people, see Boesak, "The Courage to Be Black," in *Black and Reformed,* pp. 1-19. On linking pride in oneself with pride in God, so as to reject personal degradation, see Marie Fortune, *Keeping the Faith: Questions and Answers for the Abused Woman* (New York: Harper & Row, 1987).

11. This is a familiar theme in the works of Hauerwas, Yoder, and Brueggemann already cited. All three authors struggle with the difficulty of telling Christian convictions apart from cultural assumptions, and the corresponding problem of knowing how to measure success or failure in ministry.

12. In fact, such prudence is developed chiefly by appropriating stories of practical wisdom at work in the lives of other leaders. I will discuss virtues of life on the edge in chapter 7.

13. I will look at this sort of leader in the next chapter, focusing on Paul and on opposition to apartheid in South Africa. On the ways leaders face and overcome fears of conflict in personal, social, and political spheres, see Burns, *Leadership,* pp. 49-140.

14. Burns suggests that the stronger a leader's sense of self and of positive esteem from other people, the less likely she or he is to become a power-wielder in order to gratify needs by coercion. But leaders can also be manipulated by others who take advantage of the leader's need for gratification, or prevented from exercising transforming leadership through fear of disapproval by those on whom their self-esteem depends. See *Leadership,* pp. 85-111.

15. For another story of someone whose complacency was shaken in a way that ultimately affirmed her faith and her vocation, see Mary D. Pellauer, "Invitations to the Reader," in *Sexual Assault and Abuse,* pp. vii-xxv. The rest of the book contains important material for understanding and responding to sexual violence. On this see also Fortune, *Sexual Violence* and *Keeping the Faith.*

16. On the "tearful letter" and its aftermath, see Furnish, *II Corinthians,* pp. 153-68.

6. The Temptation to Betray

1. See the chronology in Furnish, *II Corinthians*, pp. 54-55.
2. The seminal modern study on the controversies in Corinth is Dieter Georgi, *The Opponents of Paul in Second Corinthians* (Philadelphia: Fortress Press, 1986). Georgi focuses on the theological differences between Paul and his opponents, tracing their connections with Hellenistic-Jewish apologetics and assessing the roles of eschatological and Gnostic positions in the exchange. Theissen approaches the controversies from a sociological perspective in *The Social Setting of Pauline Christianity*. Theissen sees the conflict between Paul and the super-apostles as a struggle of missionary styles carrying sharply contrasting views of whether and how religious figures should be supported by the communities they visit, along with conflicting understandings of the authoritative presence of Christ, all of which leads to divergent and incompatible warrants for apostolic authority. A good summary of the controversies, as well as a detailed look at the broader context in which they occur, is found in Wayne Meeks, *The First Urban Christians* (New Haven, Conn.: Yale, 1983). Meeks sees Paul using the story of Christ as a paradigm for interpreting religious experience and tradition, and claiming that his opponents do not know or have not correctly understood the whole story. See, in addition, the relevant textual commentary in Furnish, *II Corinthians*.
3. Theissen, *The Social Setting of Pauline Christianity*, pp. 49-50.
4. On the significance of this as a status symbol in the ancient world, see Meeks, *The First Urban Christians*, pp. 71-72.
5. On these points see Georgi, "Missionary Activity in New Testament Times," in *The Opponents of Paul in Second Corinthians*, pp. 83-228, and Theissen, "The Conflict Between Itinerant Charismatics and Community Organizers," in *The Social Setting of Pauline Christianity*, pp. 40-53.
6. Thus, Meeks observes that "the letters to the Corinthians amply demonstrate the attempt to exert authority as an interpretative enterprise" (*The First Urban Christians*, p. 122).
7. Ibid., p. 138: "The most characteristic form of expression of authority for Paul, however, is the dialectical, even at times paradoxical pattern by which he tries to employ the fundamental proclamation of Christ's death and resurrection as a paradigm of authentic power." The story itself authenticates its storytellers.
8. Ibid., p. 138.
9. Although the story above is from a church context, the same dynamic can be found in any communal transmission of a story of the good. For example, the feminist critique of Western scholarship claims that the academic guardians of that story have refused to hear and take account of women's voices and experiences. On this see

Andolson et al., *Women's Consciousness, Women's Conscience*, and Gilligan, *In a Different Voice*.

10. On royal consciousness, see Brueggemann, *Prophetic Imagination*, pp. 28-43.

11. The role of the prophet in criticizing the dominant culture and energizing alternative communities is treated throughout Brueggemann, *Prophetic Imagination*. See also Brueggemann's treatment of the world-making (and thereby world-critiquing) power of the Psalms in *Israel's Praise*.

12. On twisting stories in Nazi Germany, see Stanley Hauerwas and David B. Burrell, "Self-Deception and Autobiography: Reflections on Speer's *Inside the Third Reich*," in Hauerwas, *Truthfulness and Tragedy*, pp. 82-98.

13. For two interpretations of the People's Temple experience, see Archie Smith, "An Interpretation of the People's Temple and Jonestown: Implications for the Black Church," in *The Relational Self* (Nashville: Abingdon Press, 1982), pp. 187-232, and Stanley Hauerwas, "On Taking Religion Seriously: The Challenge of Jonestown," in *Against the Nations*, pp. 91-106.

14. As we have already observed in connection with "Letter from Birmingham City Jail," Martin Luther King, Jr., spent much of his time warning against the betrayal of the gospel and of the story of America, land of the free. See also King's "Who Speaks for the South?" in *A Testament of Hope*, pp. 91-93.

15. Desmond Tutu, "Christians and Apartheid," in *Apartheid Is a Heresy*, ed. by John deGruchy and Charles Villa-Vicencio (Grand Rapids, Mich.: Eerdmans, 1983), p. 39.

16. For a good historical perspective on apartheid, see especially the essays in *Apartheid Is a Heresy* by Bosch, Maimela, and Villa-Vicencio.

17. Charles Villa-Vicencio, "An All-pervading Heresy: Racism and the 'English-speaking Churches,'" in *Apartheid Is a Heresy*, pp. 59-74.

18. Chris Loff, "The History of a Heresy," in *Apartheid Is a Heresy*, p. 20.

19. Ibid., pp. 11-20.

20. Ibid., p. 19.

21. Ibid., pp. 21-22.

22. *Die Kerkbode*, quoted in Villa-Vicencio, "An All-pervading Heresy," p. 59.

23. A. P. Treurnicht, quoted in Villa-Vicencio, "An All-pervading Heresy," pp. 59-60.

24. J. P. Vorster, quoted in Villa-Vicencio, "An All-pervading Heresy," p. 59.

25. Douglas Bax, "The Bible and Apartheid 2," in *Apartheid Is a Heresy*, p. 117.

26. See, for example, the consensus scholarship found in

Raymond Brown et al., *The Jerome Biblical Commentary* (Englewood Cliffs, N.J.: Prentice-Hall, 1968), "Genesis 10–11," p. 17; and in *Harper's Bible Dictionary*, "Babel," p. 86, and "Tower," pp. 1084-85. For a more extended commentary, see Walter Brueggemann, *Genesis* (Atlanta: John Knox, 1982).

27. Bax, "The Bible and Apartheid 2." In addition to the Tower of Babel, Bax treats four other texts commonly used in NGK arguments and thirteen texts used to argue against apartheid on scriptural grounds.

28. NGK, *Human Relations and the South African Scene in the Light of Scripture*, quoted in Bax, "The Bible and Apartheid 2," p. 118.

29. Bax, "The Bible and Apartheid," p. 116 (emphasis in original).

30. Ibid., p. 121 (emphasis in original).

31. NGK, *Human Relations and the South African Scene*, quoted in Bax, "The Bible and Apartheid 2," p. 128.

32. Bax, "The Bible and Apartheid 2," p. 129 (emphasis in original).

33. Boesak's publications include *Farewell to Innocence* (Maryknoll, N.Y.: Orbis Press, 1980); *The Finger of God* (Maryknoll, N.Y.: Orbis Press, 1982); *Walking on Thorns* (Grand Rapids, Mich.: Eerdmans, 1984), *Black and Reformed*; *If This Is Treason, I Am Guilty* (Grand Rapids, Mich.: Eerdmans, 1987); and *Comfort and Protest* (Philadelphia: Westminster Press, 1987).

34. Boesak, *Black and Reformed*, pp. 83-100.

35. Ibid., 100-110.

36. Ibid., p. 87.

37. Ibid., p. 88.

38. Ibid., p. 90.

39. Ibid., pp. 87ff.

40. Ibid., p. 92, quoting Barth, *Church Dogmatics* II/1, p. 386.

41. Ibid., pp. 92-93, quoting John Calvin, *Institutes of the Christian Faith*, Book 4, chapter 20, para. 32.

42. Ibid.

43. Ibid., p. 102.

44. Ibid.

45. Ibid., p. 103.

46. Ibid., p. 105.

47. Ibid.

48. Ibid., p. 107, quoting Calvin, *Institutes of the Christian Faith*, Book 4, chapter 17, para. 38.

49. Ibid., p. 145.

7. Living on the Edge

1. On dating II Peter and its use of Paul, see Johnson, *The Writings of the New Testament*, pp. 442-52.

2. Johnson, *The Writings of the New Testament*, p. 355. On the

uncontested authenticity of the Letter to Philemon and its relation to other New Testament writings, see pp. 350-54.

3. On Paul's attempted transformation of Philemon's world and how the letter to Philemon itself reveals much of significance about the world of early Christianity, see Petersen, *Rediscovering Paul: Philemon and the Sociology of Paul's Narrative World*, especially pp. 200-270.

4. Ibid., especially pp. 89-150.

5. Ibid., p. 270.

6. Instead of beginning with a theory of "virtue," I am treating specific virtues as they arise from stories, because there is no theoretical framework that can account for the virtues apart from some narrative, historical embodiment of them. Theoretical accounts such as those by Aristotle, Thomas, and Erikson connect virtues to human experience and social practices, but these connections make sense only as they are grounded in people's lives and made relative to an overarching story of the good. The role of the virtues in forming character appropriate to a story of the good life has been a central concern of Stanley Hauerwas; see esp. *Character and the Christian Life* and *The Peaceable Kindom*. See also Robert C. Roberts, *Spirituality and Human Emotions* (Grand Rapids, Mich.: Eerdmans, 1982); Gilbert Meilaender, *The Theory and Practice of Virtue* (Notre Dame: University of Notre Dame Press, 1984); Donald Capps, *Deadly Sins and Saving Virtues* (Philadelphia: Fortress Press, 1987); and Alasdair MacIntyre, *Whose Justice? Which Rationality?* (Notre Dame: University of Notre Dame Press, 1988).

7. On humility, see Roberta Bondi, *To Love as God Loves*, pp. 41-56, and Roberts, *Spirituality and Human Emotions*, pp. 52-75.

8. On fidelity see Richard Bondi, *Fidelity and the Good Life: Special Relations in Christian Ethics* (Ann Arbor, Mich.: University Microfilms, 1981); John S. Haughey, *Should Anyone Say Forever?* (New York: Doubleday, 1977); and Margaret Farley, *Personal Commitments*.

9. The connection between fidelity and discernment is given helpful expression by Johnson, *Decision Making in the Church*, pp. 89-100.

10. A treatment of practical wisdom as reason in the service of the good is found in MacIntyre, *Whose Justice? Which Rationality?* See also Johnson, *Decision Making in the Church*.

11. King, *Strength to Love*, pp. 9-16.

12. Prophetic vision and its companion virtue, hopeful solidarity, are recurrent themes in the work of Walter Brueggemann. In addition to works already cited, see esp. *Hopeful Imagination* (Philadelphia: Fortress Press, 1987).

13. Much of Hauerwas's work, for example, seems written in hopeful solidarity with a "church" composed of Christians past, present, and future, rather than any particular assemblage of

contemporary Christian churchgoers. See the essays collected in *Christian Existence Today.*

14. On the relativity of "justice," see MacIntyre, *Whose Justice? Which Rationality?* Early Christian monks recognized the necessity of hopeful solidarity even with those who had offended them and saw legalistic judgment as a dangerous temptation setting the judge above the sinner in a world where *all* are capable of sin. See the stories with commentary in Roberta Bondi, *To Love as God Loves.*

15. King contrasts the reality of justice in America with the hopeful solidarity envisioned by the Christian story in "Paul's Letter to American Christians," *Strength to Love,* pp. 138-46.

16. See, for example, Boesak, "Divine Obedience: A Letter to the Minister of Justice," in *Black and Reformed,* pp. 32-41.